Hov
Bestselling
Novelist

Secrets from the inside

RICHARD JOSEPH

summersdale

HOW TO BE A BESTSELLING NOVELIST

First published in longer format by Summersdale Publishers Ltd in 1997 as *Bestsellers: Top Writers Tell How*, reprinted 1997, 1998

Summersdale Publishers Ltd.
46 West Street
Chichester
West Sussex
PO19 1RP
United Kingdom

www.summersdale.com

Printed and bound in Great Britain

ISBN 1 84024 462 3

Contents

Part 3:
Adventure writers 154

RICHARD JOSEPH WAS born in London in 1940 and educated at Harrow.

Most of his career has been in the printing industry but today, he runs his own publishing company specialising in reference books for the antiquarian and second-hand trade.

He is the author of

Michael Joseph – Master of Words (1986)
Bestsellers – Top Writers Tell How (1997)

Every author, of course, has a 'beginning'
Robert Ludlum

The only way to learn to write is to write, and keep doing it until you get it damn right
Tom Clancy

Introduction

FOR EVERY AUTHOR who makes a million, there's a million authors who make very little; for a million authors who make very little, there's another million who never get published. So just what is that intangible quality that bestows fame and fortune upon the select few?

Millions dream, at some time or another in their lives, of writing a book. The more ambitious of them dream of writing a bestseller. If you have shared such dreams, read on.

The reasons that drive us to write are, of course, far too numerous to list here. For many people, however, it is simply the wish to record their own personal experiences. For the more imaginative and ambitious, it can be the dream of writing a bestseller with, perhaps, the chance of enjoying ego-boosting fame from radio and television appearances. This harmless dream is, as I have said, one that millions harbour, but only very few achieve. What are those intangible reasons by which one author is singled out from a million others for fame and glory?

To answer this question, I set out to interview a wide selection of bestselling authors. I posed a similar series of questions to each of them, and their replies, taken together, go a long way towards providing the answer. It is clear from my discussions with them, though, that each of us will draw different conclusions, depending on which replies impress us most deeply. It is the advice these authors have given that is important to all aspiring writers. They are excellent reference tips.

Although much has been published about the lives of these authors, little, if anything, has been written that explains in detail how they became such popular writers, and what it was that gave them that big break. Most press interviews reduce this fascinating aspect to just a single paragraph.

The interviews in this book occurred some years ago, but the events that led these authors to become so successful remain the same. Although the background details of these authors will not have changed, opinions and views expressed when we met might have been modified or changed during the intervening years.

Most authors do not set out to write a bestseller, and those who write for a living never really know what the formula is. More importantly, no publisher will be so rash as to state that they know for certain, either. It is all too easy to put a book's success down to luck. True, luck is a part of the answer, but attributing a book's success entirely to luck is an over-simplification.

To start with, original ideas make an important impact, and they must be such as to impress the reader. Any book has to be wanted by the public. Judging that aspect is the very crux of the mythical and magical formula, for the public's taste in reading is fickle. Then the typescript needs to be in the right publisher's hands at the appropriate moment. The publisher has to be motivated and in the right frame of mind to read it. Then, if the publisher is interested, and always assuming that author and publisher can agree terms, the book will eventually be published. But what happens then to make it a bestseller?

For example, has the author got to have a flair for advertising and public relations? Is word-of-mouth recommendation essential? And how effective is the publisher's advertising by comparison?

Bestsellers can be on any subject or theme. Historical novels like *Gone with the Wind*, even those with religious themes, like *The Robe*, humorous stories like those of P. G. Wodehouse, serious novels like *The Heart of the Matter* by Graham Greene, and romantic novels like Daphne du Maurier's *Rebecca* are all examples of successes in varied fields.

Though the theme of your book may not be important, the timing of its publication most certainly is. So the first rule, surely, is to appreciate the public's taste for reading matter. The bestselling author of twenty years ago would probably be a failure today; and today's successful author might have been a failure twenty years ago. In the main, books should either satisfy some particular hunger in the reading public, or reflect a prevailing mood (although there have been exceptions to this).

Sadly, many people who actually start their first book fail to recognise the most elementary, and most important, point of their labours. Your book, if it is ever going to be published, must in some way coincide with the public's current reading interest. You will read that the novel that achieves the rank of bestseller must rise above the level of merely competent storytelling, good writing, and skilful characterisation.

It must make people laugh or cry, or both, as well as engaging and keeping their attention and exciting their imagination. It does not have to have a conventional happy ending, but it must be a satisfying one. Publishers will tell you that few bestsellers survive to become classics, the majority being ephemeral; they blaze like rockets in the sky and tomorrow they are forgotten.

So you want to write the book of your dreams? Well, the important thing to remember is to do something about writing it, rather than just dreaming about success. Anyone who has ever thought of becoming a writer would do well to note Arthur Hailey's comment:

> Get on with it. There are people who 'talk book', and there are people who 'write book'; talking writers, and writing writers.

ays write from the heart.
- Strong central character
- Sub-plot?

THINGS TO CONSIDER
• Finding an agent
• Overcoming writer's block
 riter should always
  a notebook & pen.

Part 1

General
fiction

Jilly Cooper

How To Stay Married, How to Survive From Nine to Five, Jolly Super, Men & Super Men, Riders, Rivals, Polo, The Man Who Made Husbands Jealous, Appassionata, Pandora, Prudence and 33 others.

AMONG THE MYRIAD colourful books that can be seen on almost every bookseller's display stands are those of the prolific writers of romance. When sex is mentioned, it is usually with very genteel phrases. On the other hand, a number of authors have made a lot by writing good, raunchy love scenes, creating what today are known as 'bonkbusters'. And Jilly Cooper must rank amongst the best-known.

She is one author who, even in her early career as a writer, was well-known to millions of readers. Jilly would be the first to admit that her fame was helped in the beginning by the wide audience, gained over the years from regular contributions to national newspapers, and from appearances on television. What is more, appearing on national television programmes ensured that her humour and repartee were appreciated by many more people than are regular book buyers; a rare ability in a writer. I was to learn that it was her witty conversation that originally led her to become a writer in the first place. So as I travelled to interview her at her country home in Bisley, Gloucestershire, I was also ready to be entertained.

She lives and works in what some might call a mansion, but which is in reality a house that was originally built, more than seven hundred years ago, as a place for monks to practise their chanting. From her drawing-room there are uninterrupted views across a small valley, carpeted with open fields. A peaceful environment which many would envy, and an ideal one in which to write; one step outside, and you are away from 'civilisation' – and the telephone.

People tend to remember Jilly as a flirtatious blonde, often to be seen at parties with a glass in her hand and a gaggle of men around her. Don't be fooled. Despite that extrovert party image, she has been described as both 'insecure and ludicrously sensitive': characteristics of any successful creative writer. Jilly had the good fortune to have been born into an extremely happy upper middle class family who came from Yorkshire. After the last war, her father, Bill Sallitt, who had been one of the Army's youngest brigadiers, returned to Yorkshire, moving into a splendid Georgian house which was partly used as his office. It was the ideal setting, with seven acres of fields, ideal for her ponies, and not short of other amenities with a swimming pool, tennis and squash courts.

On arrival, I was warmly greeted by both Jilly and her dogs. Coffee was instantly provided, and we adjourned to the drawing-room, which seemed to double as a library. Books were everywhere, from floor to ceiling. My eyes searched the shelves for a copy of *Riders*, one of her better known novels, which I thought would be a good starting-point for our discussion. So it proved, for as I complimented her, she began to talk about the book with animated and bubbly enthusiasm.

Soon after the book had been published in hardback, I had to go to speak at a literary dinner in Exeter. The guests included many paperback publishers, and elite members of the publishing world and booksellers. I noticed the long faces and dark mutterings, particularly from the women. I discovered afterwards that they had just seen the cover of the British paperback edition and were very far from happy about the design. They said it was far too sexy and sexist for their markets and that it demeaned women by having a man's hand on a woman's bottom. I myself was slightly startled to begin with by the cover, but I soon got used to it and now I think it is a great cover. Every other country has used it on their editions, except for the American edition.

Jilly then showed me the American paperback edition as it was finally published. The cover had a round hole cut into it and was somewhat reminiscent of *Dynasty* – certainly not the image that Jilly would have preferred. *Riders*, her twenty-seventh book, was published in 1985, but it took her over fifteen years to finish it. She says she is a slow writer, but not that slow! In fact the only copy of the first final manuscript was inadvertently left on a London bus, and was never seen again – an author's nightmare come true. Jilly had to write the book all over again; at the time she was living in London, with frequent parties and people dropping in – not an ideal situation.

I wrote a lot at school, but never got beyond the third chapter. I used to also write romantic stories and plays, but most of all, I wanted to be a journalist. I used to see these men in macintoshes and hats, clustering around and interviewing beautiful film stars at airports, and I wanted to be one of the men in macintoshes.

But I never could have written long books before I was married – because my love life was always getting in the way. I settled down after I was married, but life does tend to get in the way of writing, doesn't it? Actually, I find writing incredibly difficult, each article for *The Sunday Times* or *The Mail on Sunday* was re-drafted and drafted at least a dozen times, and *Riders* took at least seven drafts.

Jilly's bubbly, extrovert personality is in many ways the opposite of other writers I have met. After leaving school, she went through numerous jobs, from secretary to reporter, though she recounted her career with humour:

I was sacked from twenty-two jobs. I was so incompetent as a temporary typist, the letters I did on Monday came back by Wednesday, and I was out that day. I've been a switchboard operator, advertising copywriter – that was a nightmare – but I eventually settled in a job with the *Middlesex Independent* when I was eighteen. I actually stayed with them for two years, but I nearly didn't last the first day. I reported a wedding and got the bride married to the best man!

I always wanted to get to Fleet Street – there were riches to be had there – and with lots of boozy lunches.

But it was later, when she was working at Collins, the publishers, that the opportunity to start writing occurred. Each author's introduction into the world of writing is, of course, unique, but once they have got started, it is that intangible quality that singles one writer out for real fame and fortune which is so intriguing. Jilly was working in the company's publicity department at the time, helping to entertain guests at all those parties held to promote books. This left her with time on her hands, and a friend at Odhams asked her if she would like to help edit a new teenage magazine. It was during this period that she realised that many of the stories submitted for publication were really very poor. In despair, she thought she could perhaps write better stories.

She succeeded surprisingly quickly, getting five stories published in other magazines, including *Woman's Own*. She was living in Fulham with, at one time, twenty-two cats, and not being enamoured with the chores of housework, home was in a permanent state of delightful chaos. When she told a friend that she was thinking of writing a piece about housework, she received the cutting reply, 'But you don't do any!'

> I went to a dinner party and met Godfrey Smith, editor of *The Sunday Times* colour magazine, and started to talk about being a young wife and how awful it was, working all day, shopping all one's lunch hour, rushing home, cleaning the house, cooking one's husband's dinner, making love all night, getting up in the morning, going to work, shopping all lunch hour, getting home, doing the housework, cooking one's husband's dinner, making love all night, and after six months one collapsed from exhaustion. Godfrey thought this was so funny that he asked me to write a piece. I wrote it and *The Sunday Times* colour magazine

accepted it and gave me one hundred pounds. That week I was offered nine jobs and one of them was a column on *The Sunday Times*, another to write my first book.

Just what is it, apart from her skill as a writer, that singled her out for such huge success? I noticed that a number of her books carry her portrait, perhaps cashing in on her many appearances on television and contributions in national newspapers. She has earned what is called a 'high-profile' or 'public-relations' image, which is just one aspect of marketing books. Jilly has an immensely charming way of talking about so many varied subjects that it's no wonder that for some years she frequently appeared on television chat shows, or quiz games; perceptive enough to ask all the right questions, and witty enough to be remembered by the viewer long after the programme had been broadcast. She is very direct and her remarks can be very incisive. As a writer, she is also uninhibited in her attitude to sex. She believes that sex can be fun, and enjoys ribbing the stuffy English about their inhibitions.

Her press, and then her television appearances have undoubtedly helped her career as a novelist.

Unlike writers such as Francis or Herriot, however, her work does embrace a number of literary genres. *Emily*, *Harriet*, *Octavia* and *Imogen* rank as romantic novels; *How to Survive From Nine To Five* and *Men and Super Men* – humour; *Class*, a send up of the English Class system – satire; *The Common Years* recounts life as she saw it; *Animals In War* is history. None of her early romantic novels became out-and-out international blockbusters, but later titles such as *Riders*, *Rivals*, *Polo*, *The Man Who Made Husbands Jealous*, and *Appassionata* have become the 'blockbusters' which both publishers and authors strive to achieve.

Her husband Leo is a publisher in his own right. Many successful authors have close links with the publishing world, but it is not essential; and becoming a journalist does not automatically result in becoming a writer of bestsellers. Strong and close links with publishers should increase an author's confidence, but she told me that her books have always been written with colossal despair and anguish; and she believed that each one was going to be a disaster until it was finished.

I wondered how Jilly reacted to reviews of her books. Having been a journalist it seems that if they are very critical, she could exact revenge very easily.

> In the past I may have been treated lightly because I was a journalist and maybe there was a flicker at the back of their minds that if they were nasty, I would retaliate, but it is such a long time since I have been a journalist that I don't think it worries them anymore, particularly bearing in mind some of the savage reviews when *Appassionata* first came out. But I think you should try and accept criticism and read reviews carefully because it is very possible they may be right and you may learn something from them.

I was prompted to ask whether the rewards from her writing had made any real difference to her life.

> The trouble for writers is they don't get taxed at source and so if you are given a great whack of money, you tend to spend it, or give it away to people who desperately need things and then the horror comes when you have to pay the tax. Equally, you may have a brilliant year when a book does terribly well, and then the next year

> you don't do nearly so well and you have to pay
> the tax on a brilliant year.

This was not the response I had expected; if any
author has fame and fortune suddenly thrust upon
them, this is certainly a salutary warning.

I have asked everyone interviewed for this book
what advice they would give to an aspiring author.
Not that such advice should be taken literally, but
it does in a way reflect what factors have helped, in
the authors' own opinions, to make them successful.
So what was Jilly's advice?

> Without doubt, keep a diary. From the day you
> are born, keep a diary, because we all forget
> things so quickly. I didn't start until I was thirty
> and I missed so much.
>
> When writing, keep your sentences short.
> Use colour as much as possible, and use the five
> senses as much as possible. Just try to explain
> what it was like to be there. Journalistic rules
> are very good. I think journalists write lousy
> English, but readable prose. I'd always rather
> write readable prose and lousy English. Except
> it can date you in twenty years or so.

I never went to a university. You learn to think logically there and write literary English, but you won't necessarily become a good writer.

I think if I wanted someone to learn to write, I'd send them to a newspaper for two years. No longer, because you become too hardened after that time.

With 11 million sales in the UK alone, her advice is worth noting.

Roald Dahl

Roald Dahl was a master wordsmith, but neither he nor his readers would have believed it from his school reports. From the age of fourteen, the annual comments about his ability in English Composition were consistently awful. They suggested that he could not put a sentence together, let alone write an acceptable essay.

He left school at eighteen, preferring not to go on to university but to join the exciting world of big business instead. He also yearned to travel overseas, and secured himself a job with the eastern staff of the Shell Oil Company, though for the first few years he was based at their offices in London.

Dahl was in Africa when the war broke out, joining the RAF to become a fighter pilot. His real break came unexpectedly in 1942 when he was invalided home and then sent to Washington DC, as an Assistant Air Attaché. He hadn't been in Washington many days when he had an unexpected visitor to his office at the British Embassy, C. S. Forester, an author widely known for those tales of seafaring derring-do featuring his hero, Horatio Hornblower.

Forester explained that he was writing things about Britain for the American papers and magazines. He had a contract with the *Saturday Evening Post* which would publish any story that he wrote, and he believed that Dahl had a story about combat-flying to tell. They went for lunch and Dahl started to tell Forester about the time in Libya when he attempted to land his Gloster Gladiator in the desert, sustaining injuries and burns. He later flew Hurricanes and took part in fierce air-to-air combat in Greece where he claimed several victories.

Recounting the story, making notes and eating all at the same time proved rather difficult, so Dahl agreed to go away and write notes for Forester. That night, he began to write, and as he did so, he became totally absorbed in describing the events. He wrote freely for the next five hours. The next day he had it typed out and sent off to Forester. He received a letter, which said:

'You said you were going to send me notes... you have sent me a complete story. My agent, Harold Matson, has sent it to the *Saturday Evening Post* untouched, with my recommendation... and they accepted it at once. Their cheque is enclosed.'

Dahl, as a writer of fiction par excellence, set down seven basic qualities that any aspiring author should have:

1. You should have a lively imagination.

2. You should be able to write well. By that I mean you should be able to make a scene come alive in the reader's mind. Not everybody has this ability. It is a gift, and you either have it or you don't.

3. You must have stamina. In other words, you must be able to stick to what you are doing and never give up, for hour after hour, day after day, week after week and month after month.

4. You must be a perfectionist. That means you must never be satisfied with what you have written until you have rewritten it again and again, making it as good as you possibly can.

5. You must have strong self-discipline. You are working alone. No one is employing you. No one is around to give you the sack if you don't turn up for work, or to tick you off if you start slacking.

6. It helps a lot if you have a keen sense of humour. It is not essential when writing for grown-ups, but for children, it's vital.

7. You must a have a degree of humility. The writer who thinks that his work is great is heading for trouble.

Paul Erdman

The Billion Dollar Sure Thing, The Silver Bears, The Crash of '79, The Panic of '89, The Last Days of America, The Palace, What Next?, The Set-Up and others.

HIS PUBLISHING COMPANY once proclaimed that 'Paul Erdman is one of America's most sought after economists'. Clearly, he is an author of bestsellers with a difference.

He writes what he calls 'financial thrillers'; anyone who can accurately predict, as he did, a major crash in a nation's stockmarket, is almost bound to captivate the attention of financial 'experts'. For those not conversant with the money markets, he accurately predicted the colossal fall in share values in October 1987. Before the event, he made no secret of the fact that he was selling all his stockholdings. This public demonstration caused many more people than just the experts to sit up and take notice. Nowadays, people hang on his every word, and personal fortunes can often be made or lost from the very inflection of his voice.

To interview him, I travelled to San Francisco, where we lunched at one of the city's most prestigious hotels, the Huntingdon. Hitherto, I had held most of my interviews in the authors' homes, where they had felt relaxed and at ease. I need not have worried about this meeting either, for Paul knew almost everybody there.

Where, then, did he start his writing career? Born in Germany, he fled from there in the 1930s to Canada, where his schooling put him on the road to success. He explained:

> Yes, I was good at English, but I'll tell you what. I had been brought up in Great School, in Canada, and if you came from Canada at that time, then by definition you were better in English than anyone in the United States!
>
> I was also good at languages, I had six years of Ancient Greek, six years of Latin and was always rather adept at that. It's a game, languages, you know. I enjoyed playing that game...
>
> I was also very good at mathematics, but that is another story. I remember when I sat the exams, you could walk out when you had finished, and I would finish a one hour paper after ten minutes!

Obviously then, he showed himself to be talented with figures, but did he ever believe that he would one day become a famous writer? Was he so good that he was encouraged by others to write?

No, no. I had no ambition whatsoever to be such, but I was, like, the editor of my Lutheran prep school newspaper, and editor of the Year Book. This was just because – I mean I was also Captain of the Debating Team. Perhaps that helped.

I also graduated *summa cum laude* from the University of Basle, where there was a certain, I guess you know, aura of qualification. Nevertheless I could have graduated the lowest qualification in that grading system, and if this 'professor' had insisted that it [his dissertation] would be published, it would have been published. I think, though, that this was not based on merit. It was a full doctorial dissertation, but it had to be condensed really for publication in this book form, because you have an awful lot of foot-noting... [It was entitled *Swiss-American Economic Relations*.]

I did get some flak on this, by the way. It was very interesting. The Federal Council, the seven-man council which runs the collective presidency of Switzerland, wanted to block the publication of this [the dissertation], or so I believe. Because there were certain elements of what they [the Swiss] had done in World War Two and subsequently... Most of which was not public knowledge and they certainly did not want it published – and my doctor father, to his great credit, said, 'I'll publish and you can be damned', which is what happened.

It sold out, but that does not mean much because they would only print two thousand, and one thousand nine hundred and ninety-nine would be bought by libraries, and my mother bought the other one!

No, I was never encouraged, in fact years later, after I had taken my degree in Georgetown, I decided to study in Europe. I went by sea, a ten-day voyage from New York to Le Havre; the North Atlantic weather was perfect. All you do is eat and drink all day.

On one occasion, I picked a good deck-chair, and the husband half of a couple next to me was a literary agent and so I thought, well, I mean, this is the time to peddle my memories...

He said, 'Wait until you are forty and know something, then write something', and he was absolutely right. That's almost the cliché, but that's the first time anybody had told me that, and I thought, what the hell, here I am, twenty-four, and on the marvellous liner, heading for Le Havre. I mean, there's a budding Hemingway here somewhere.

He smashed that daydream, and I think that's the only time I have ever, as they say in America these days, been verbalised.

One of my lasting impressions of this financial genius is that he displayed such a casual attitude to writing. He almost gives the impression that he is totally unaffected by all the fuss, and it is not until you read just how much he is earning from writing that you realise the size of his readership. In February 1987, the *Financial World* reported that he was earning anything from $500,000 to $1 million from each of his books. They even quoted him saying: 'I'm now making more than ever. This one, *The Panic of '89*, will earn me a minimum of two million dollars.'

That may sound rather blasé, but then he has always talked in millions, no matter what the currency. Bibliographical sketches all mention his career in banking, so to talk in such terms seems quite natural. Erdman's own description of his career is remarkably candid:

> I wrote a similar book, but in German and after that, I went on to the Stafford Research Institute out here [California] and used to write little essays on what your parents are going to look like in twenty years and stuff like that... Then I started my own bank in Switzerland and all that old story where I end up in gaol!
>
> I'd better explain. In the fall of 1970, in Switzerland, where there is no habeas corpus [which requires anybody who detains a person in custody to produce the accused in court. It prevents people being imprisoned on mere suspicion or being left in prison indefinitely without trial], I was stuck there for a while – nine months, in fact. This was in 'investigative incarceration' and there was no way to get out at all. My embassy tried and my contact said, 'Look, Erdman, confess to something and we'll get you out. You are a young kid...'
>
> Are you kidding? So there I was, and I thought to pass the time, I'd write something, such as I'd done earlier. These two books about economics but, of course, you don't have research facilities

in gaol, even in Swiss gaols. So I gave that up.

Then I thought about some of those ideas which I had had in the economic realm; for example, as a result of the Vietnam War which we had just gone through, the inevitable outcome would have to be a decline in the dollar and a rise in the price of gold. I took some of these themes which had never really been addressed in action and put them in a novel and that was precisely the origin of it. The motivation was simply boredom in gaol.

Only because of these peculiar circumstances, where you have literally nothing to lose, you can't make a fool of yourself, nobody is going to read it, I had a go. I would never have attempted to write a novel, because all of us grow up reading novels and you have enormous respect for people who do that.

I'm much too much of a realist, and I know that the odds on somebody like myself, in those circumstances, having a novel published are, I would say, a million to one. Maybe more than that. No, it was just a way to pass the time.

Without wishing to appear cynical, I wondered if the thought had ever struck him that it might have been quite difficult for him to return straightaway to the world of finance after having been imprisoned on suspicion of fraud, and that writing might therefore have been a welcome occupation and an alternative source of income. I also wondered how his incarceration in a seventeenth-century dungeon in Basle ended? Was there a court case, or did the authorities give up their investigations?

Well, I subsequently got out of there with the help of some friends and governments, and a couple of years later, I was sentenced *in absentia* to nine years in gaol over there.

The charge was fraud, not fraud that I stole anything, but fraud that the balance sheets of my bank did not reflect reality. This was because my commodity and foreign-exchange dealers had suffered losses which they kept in the drawer and which were not reflected in the balance sheets. In essence, this amounts to deceiving the public of its money.

You know, because of the immense amounts that can be involved the penalty rises with the value. For twenty thousand francs, you get like three months, if it's fifty thousand, you get half a year; if fifty million, the sky's the limit!

Paul went on to describe his experiences 'inside'. His single cell had a bath, and he was allowed to have his typewriter so that he could write his 'scribblings'. He could order any meal from any restaurant and have it delivered, provided he paid for it, and he had wine from his cellar. He was also able to keep himself fully informed, for he had *The Times*, *Financial Times* and the *Herald Tribune* delivered, and he had television and radio as well; in fact, he could obtain anything that he needed, if he could pay for it.

When he finally got out of prison, he eventually moved to the United States of America, but what happened immediately after his return to freedom?

> A friend of mine, one of the famous art dealers in Switzerland, had a marvellous villa on the hills overlooking Lugarno, and he said (and we never stay at people's homes, I don't like that), he said, 'Look, we have this place, we have servants and everything. Why don't you go down there and get over this thing?'
>
> So down we went [Paul and his wife, Helly] and after a couple of weeks, we got a phone call down there from the head of the *Wall Street*

Journal in Europe. I'd been feeding him material for years and he said, 'I'm headed for New York with my wife, Margaret, and I hear that you've been "scribbling away at something".'

I asked them to join us for dinner that Saturday up at this villa. There was some sort of village festival on that weekend; Italian type of thing, on the church square with lots of heavy wine and sometime during the early hours the subject turned to my 'scribblings' and he said, 'Well look, I'm going in to see Charlie Scribner [the New York publisher] shortly and whatever you have got, I'll throw the transcript at him.' So we xeroxed the thing the next morning and he took it to New York.

In the interim I moved to England, moved to Buckinghamshire and got a phone call one day from Scribner's in New York, who said they were interested but would like to see more.

They were very encouraging about this, so I did write more, and got this thing up to the halfway point and sent it over there. Then the president of Scribner's ends up on my doorstep three days later and said, 'We'd like to buy this thing', and gave me a very minor advance of five thousand dollars. So I finished this up, and then things started to happen.

That was in the spring of 1973. Then there was an agent in London called Molly Watters, she had heard about this and came to our house in Gerrards Cross, in Buckinghamshire.

She went away and flogged these rights to France, to Paris Match; to publishers in Germany and Italy, before it had come out anywhere. Then it came out in New York and hit the bestseller list within four weeks, and stayed on for quite a while. I forget how long, but it went to number one actually for a week, I think. It must have been on the list for twenty or thirty weeks. There we were and all thanks to Ray Vicar, the chief correspondent for the *Wall Street Journal*.

The reason why this book, *The Billion Dollar Sure Thing*, grabbed so much attention at the time lay in the basis for the plot. Erdman's theme was international intrigue in the aftermath of the Vietnam War, and especially attempts to influence the price of gold and the value of the dollar. In reality, both had hit extremes of value in the year the book came out. The novel appeared to be very close to the truth and timing is all-important to success.

Paul's advance against the future royalties of *The Billion Dollar Sure Thing* had been only $5,000, but with the rights sales in Europe and the book's instant appearance on the bestseller lists, he would have recovered the advance and started earning more royalties very quickly. Whereas $5,000 would have been great news to most aspiring authors, it has to be remembered that Paul Erdman was one of Europe's highly paid executives. He had a PhD in economics, had founded a bank and had gained, for an American, an enormous amount of financial experience in Switzerland.

Now, though, he had suddenly become an established author and was, no doubt, tempted to write another book.

> It was intended to be a one-shot deal that had been thrust on me by circumstances. As I said, I was doing it out of boredom and all of a sudden I was encouraged to finish the sucker and so, well, I thought, well, why not?
>
> In fact, I only finished this thing because I was supposed to go on a long extended trip through the Middle and Far East and I remember how my wife Helly said, 'Look, if you do that, you'll never finish this thing. Right. Stay home and finish it.'
>
> She helped me then, and helps me now. In

two ways. Firstly, she reads it, and I trust her judgement; if she says it's good, I go on. If she says it's bad, I say 'What the hell do you know?' And go back and forget it.

Secondly, we did not have word processors then and I type, but not well. And so she would always retype it.

With *The Billion Dollar Sure Thing* a bestseller, was he asked to write another immediately?

Yeah. *Silver Bears* with Scribner's, but another publisher, Pocket Books, picked up the paperback rights on that one. I liked this book, and I thought it was funny, you know? And very light-hearted and amusing.

So, granted that, in the financial world, he was quite well-known, and with *The Billion Dollar Sure Thing* a success, did Scribner's have to promote him and *Silver Bears* – with television, radio interviews, book signings, and all the other activities of the bestselling author?

Well, Pocket Books was and is part of Simon and Schuster, and they were becoming the big boy on the block. Public relations and marketing are important and Scribner's being a small house, with a great literary tradition, has not got a great marketing tradition. Pocket Books fed them on the first book, I think, with seventy-five-thousand or one-hundred-thousand bucks, which was a lot of money then, just to market this thing. This impressed me and that's why subsequently I switched from Scribner's to Simon and Schuster.

I am always fascinated to find out whether authors who suddenly find fame and fortune (well, relatively speaking in Paul Erdman's case), bother to keep all the press cuttings and memorabilia?

No. I used to have a big cardboard box. Helly always used to ask, 'Why do you keep those things?' I really don't know. Everybody else keeps scrap-books, at least I can have a cardboard box. And about five years ago, we burned the box, because, I think, we needed the room. Now we never keeps reviews, we burn them.

Today we have computers which store all this stuff, so you don't need my box.

Reviews are important, depending on where they come from and who writes them. If it is somebody that you know, with some repute, you should pay attention. If it's good, I wouldn't pay too much attention, but if it's bad, or it includes some suggestions as to what you might consider doing next, you should listen to that. No doubt about it. Just to say that all reviewers are out to get you, are bad, is nonsense.

Other authors I have interviewed disregard reviews, though, if they are honest with themselves I am sure they would agree that this form of publicity can be very hurtful to the ego.

What are Erdman's views about other methods of promotion, then?

I think there are two phases of this; if one does not lead to the other then forget it. First, you do radio and television interviews, and that should promote word of mouth. I'm sure you've heard this a million times. If word of mouth does not pick up on that then forget it. You are flogging a dead horse.

But he started his writing career as a well-known banker, even if one forgets the 'fame' of having been in gaol. Surely that gave him a head start?

> Absolutely. Especially, not only as a financial man, but in gaol. In Switzerland, it is a very sexy concept. It was a prime reason, but I don't know whether it's the prime reason.
>
> I would be fibbing if I didn't agree that I had acquired a certain notoriety... Financial people never went to gaol, you know, and this guy had not only ended up in a Swiss gaol, but had a bank, he must really know something.
>
> I know my stuff in this field. It was like you have seen with [Tom] Clancy. He is a man who knows military hardware and his readers sensed this. And they said, 'Look, you've got to read this guy. He knows what he's talking about; knows his hardware.' And that is what has happened here.

As to Paul being a full-time writer, rather than a financier, he thought:

> Being a writer was much easier. You don't have to be responsible for employees; you don't have

> to be responsible for other people's money
> either and you don't have to answer to a board
> of directors. As a writer, you answer only to
> yourself.
>
> If somebody screws up, it's only your fault!
> The only time you suffer, as a writer, is when
> you are too lazy to see that you do what you
> are supposed to do.

Our conversation then turned to that important, and often taxing question as to what title to give your work. Paul was very succinct:

> A bad title can hurt you, and a good title can help
> you somewhat. *The Crash of '79* was a uniquely
> good title. But titles do not good books make.

Each author has his or her favourite book, one that was easiest to write, or that secured gratifying reviews and subsequent sales, or that they just like the best. Paul is no exception, for he told me that out of seven or so thrillers, his favourite was *The Crash of '79*, and he enthused at length about the fun he derived from writing it. If, as he said, he thoroughly enjoyed writing and the subsequent results, did he write what he wanted to, or what he believed the public, and the film moguls, might want?

> No, I write what I want to write. I write what I think has 'legs'; in other words, a story which can end up as a full-fledged novel, so it has to have a story with sufficient strength of its own, with sufficient opportunity for sub-plots and so forth...

But in taking his story and developing it into a novel, was he aware of any weaknesses in writing, and if so, did he take these into account? He grinned:

> Yeah. I have many weaknesses. I mean, God's gift to the literary world I am not. I think my primary weakness is character development; where there is a certain set of standards, I would say that one expects characters to be developed much more fully than mine are.

So when he planned his books, did he do so in great detail, or just take a theme and go for it?

Neither. I want to know where it starts, the beginning, the middle and end. A two-page memo to myself suffices for that, but then when I write, if I'm smart, instead of sitting down and waiting, like you're suggesting, the better way to do it is to take a shower and then get up, write yourself the outline for the day so you have your two-page memo, the beginning, middle and end, but also the sequences you outline.

This, I thought, sounded like advice to others.

I've never given advice to people. I usually say forget about it. That sounds crass, but I'd forget about it. Unless somebody, someone with real brains and experience in the publishing field, suggests it, forget about it.

If somebody writes something, the first ten pages will tell you whether it's there or not. Don't you agree? If it isn't, don't push it, because you probably have not got it.

To write, I think you have to be gifted a bit. To write is not something you learn at Iowa State University, it is something you are able to do, but on top of that, increasingly, you have to know what you are writing about. I think it helps to have enough money because then you can write when you choose and you are not under the gun.

I think you have to produce these things at your leisure, but if you do that you'll write a book every hundred years, so there have to be incentives, but not just to make money. That might sound idealistic... .

Did he think that anyone who wants to write has to do something else for a living? Does that help?

No. I think that hinders. I think that if you want to write, you have to be able to get up in the morning, thinking full-time about that novel, in your mind's eye. You are seeing the scene developing. If you have a business on the side you can't do that. So I think that it is an enormous disadvantage to have to be doing something else to make money.

I posed my last question: what was the key to the success of his books? Was it perhaps the financial uncertainties of the future?

No. I think it's the way you tell the story that sells. And my stories are about a world which is very intriguing, a world of high finance, and a world of intrigue involving the names that they read about, say, in the newspapers every day, the Rockefellers, the Kissingers, the heads of these big banks; and in my case, they are told by a guy who knows these people.

Write what you know about. That is sound advice.

James Herriot

To most people, writing letters is a tedious chore, but not to Herriot. In his younger days he wrote numerous letters home, and his father always enjoyed receiving them for their vivid descriptions of events and sights. Then one day his father suggested that since his letters were so good, he ought to think about writing a book.

Perhaps it was his father who sowed the seed. As Herriot explained, he thought he had to start somewhere, and writing short stories became his first goal.

They kept coming back with regular monotony and it's a terrible thing when you hear the postman pushing the rejected manuscript through the letterbox. It lands on the floor with such a sickening thud. Again, again and again, they were returned. I grew to hate that sound. And there wasn't one word of encouragement with any of them.

I realised that, though my style was improving, the subjects were wrong. So I returned to stories that I knew something about. When I rewrote them, and sent my first manuscript of a book off though, that was different. It wasn't immediately returned. Days passed; and the days became weeks, and still no rejection. I thought it must be under serious consideration, and I was delighted. But nothing of the sort. Eighteen months later, a reply came, 'Sorry, our lists are full, but we have sent it to our subsidiary.' Another six months went by, and then they, too, said their lists were full. Bitter, bitter disappointment. So I put the work back into my drawer and tried to forget all about it. I had tried to write and failed. As the months passed, my wife chided me to do as I had read and send it off to a literary agent. Well, eventually I did, and one week later, their memorable reply was, 'We'll have no trouble getting this published.'

An astute editor spotted a similarity with Richard Gordon's *Doctor in the House*. There were similar anecdotal qualities but linked to animals, and books about animals always sold well. It was well written, too, and needed virtually no editing.

I wrote my books because of a compulsion to make some record of a fascinating era in veterinary practice. I wanted to tell people what it was like to be an animal doctor in those days before penicillin, and about the things that made me laugh on my daily rounds, working in conditions which now seem primitive. I suppose I started out with the intention of just writing a funny book, but as I progressed I found that there were so many other things that I wanted to say. I wanted to tell about the sad things too; about the splendid old characters among the animal owners of that time and about the magnificent Yorkshire countryside which at all times was the backdrop to my work.

They say we should not live in the past... But to me, my past is a sweet, safe place to be, and through the medium of these stories I shall spend a little time there now and then.

When I was in full spate, I would arrive home late at night, probably from helping a cow to calve, sit down in front of the television [he worked with the set switched on; he liked to be with his family, not shut away in another room] and I squeezed my efforts into the last half hour each day. My job as a vet was an exhausting

one; often twenty-four hours a day, seven days
a week, with no Bank Holidays off, and often not
Christmas Day, either. I have never written for
more than half an hour in my life. Writing to me
only occupies a teeny wee bit of my life. And to
be truthful, I hate writing. I wouldn't like the idea
of writing all day at all.

With all the hype that there is in publishing today,
it seems strange that there wasn't a launch party for
his first book. No big celebrations: just the quiet
publication of the work of a very modest vet. And
he only got £200 as his first advance against royalties.
At first, sales of *If Only They Could Talk* were very
modest. Herriot's editor suggested that he should
write another. In the meantime the publishers sold
the American rights to St. Martin's Press in America.
They also believed the book to be a winner and, two
years later, combined his second book, *It Shouldn't
Happen to a Vet*, with the first to create *All Creatures
Great and Small*. St. Martin's Press had, it seems,
taken a gamble, sending the first chapter, bound
up as a dummy book, to most of the important
booksellers. Sales suddenly started to escalate: and
what happens in America sooner or later happens

here. Sales in this country started to rise too, and then the books came out in paperback. It was like lighting the blue touch paper of a firework. Sales took off, and the books began to appear in the bestseller lists. Herriot enthused:

> All down to the Americans, you see. That book sold millions, word for word, just as I had written it. The Americans are crazier about animals than we are, and anything that you write about animals is bound to sell.

If he had to sum up his success and provide tips for others, what would he say?

> There's a lot of luck in becoming a successful writer. I like a good read, and there are so many people who can write well. In those early days, I used to read Conan Doyle, Dickens and Hemingway with enthusiasm. I also enjoy reading theatre critics, for they write far better than I can. They express themselves so well. Above all, if someone wants to become a bestselling author, they must write, write, and keep writing.
> I tried to develop a chatty, conversational style.

Lightweight stuff. Once I got the hang of that, it just went.

Don't use too many adjectives, that's important. And there's another little tip, which may not be the whole thing. Let the reader discover for himself. Don't describe too much. Don't say, 'He was a tall, fair-haired man', just say, 'he brushed his fair hair back off his forehead.' Corny, I know, but it illustrates the point. The reader likes to find the character out for himself.

I had a classical education, which I think helped. It makes you reject the horrible things in your writing. But there have been a hell of a lot of writers who haven't been well educated. And it's better not to be rich. A hungry writer is more likely to succeed.

You've got to want to write because no one has said before what you want to say; and only you have experienced it; and you believe that the stories are worth telling.

Alan Dean Foster

The Tar-Aiym Krang, Bloodhype, Icerigger,
Star Wars: The Approaching Storm and
novelisations for Star Trek Logs, Aliens and
The Chronicles of Riddick, Lost and Found
as well as more than sixty other science-fiction
novels. Worldwide sales in excess of 20 million.

ALAN DEAN FOSTER lives in the USA, but in Arizona
rather than amongst the jet-setters of Hollywood,
Florida, or New York. Both he and his wife, JoAnn,
like their privacy, which is one reason that they live
in a small historic town.

Their modern and spacious home is built from
bricks salvaged from a turn-of-the-century brothel.
He keeps an assortment of pets: three dogs, six cats
and a salamander, suggesting that this master writer
of scary science-fiction is no average soul. He clearly
prefers the quiet life, for he told me that peace is
essential to allow his imagination to run free to create
those ingenious and original stories. He is one of
America's top science-fiction writers.

Unlike many of the other authors I have interviewed, who began as part-time writers, he started writing at twenty-two, and has continued on steadily ever since. The majority of his titles average approximately 150,000 sales, and that's just in the USA. Nevertheless, he remains a very modest man, and eschews most of the trappings of stardom. I wanted to know just what made science-fiction his main choice as a subject. His formative years really did play a major part in shaping his career, and in choosing his subject, as he explained:

> If you think about childhood, a lot of things that happen then eventually make an appearance in your work one way or another, and often in surprising ways. For example, I was a big dinosaur fan when I was a kid. Now dinosaurs have kind of come full circle, popularity-wise, and I suspect that my descriptions of alien creatures in alien worlds has to do with my fascination as a child with a world that once was.
>
> Also, as a kid I was the proverbial skinny egg-head, yesterday's term for the more contemporary 'nerd'. As one of the underdogs, I always rooted for others like myself, whether they were human or otherwise. So when I began

the series of books known as the *Universe of the Commonwealth*, I placed among a number of other intelligent alien races I invented, one patterned on oversized insects. These Thranx turn out to be our best friends 'out there'. They are a reflection of one of my favourite literary devices, which involves turning the expected into the unexpected. Mankind has been warring with insects ever since we've been farming; giant bugs are a staple of cheapo Hollywood horror films, and so I thought it would be interesting if among all the intelligent species we might encounter, the ones it turns out that we get along with the best resemble our most persistent ancient enemies.

All that arises out of my being on the side of the underdog as a child.

Another childhood influence, and a particular powerful one, came from reading the works of the great American comic book writer and artist, Carl Barks. Barks created Uncle Scrooge, the only senior-citizen hero in the history of comic books (as opposed to the daily newspaper strips). While my adolescent contemporaries were eagerly devouring the superhero exploits of the likes of Superman and Batman and the Flash, I never saw the point in rooting for someone who already had super powers.

Scrooge McDuck, on the other hand, is a seventy-year-old short person with feathers. His vision is short and so he has to wear glasses. He walks with a cane and suffers from a variety of old-age ailments, from bursitis to lumbago. Yet in spite of these handicaps, he travels all over the world looking after his assorted business interests, has marvellous adventures, and through the strength of his will and intelligence, always outwits (never outmuscles) the bad guys. Not only is he a hero who wins by using his brains, he's an old hero.

What I drew from this, was that old age is not to be feared – quite a lesson for a pre-adolescent. As a result, it strongly affected the portrayal of older characters in my own work. I like to think they're less stereotyped, more active, more involved in advancing the plot as opposed to standing around like antiquated window dressing.

That comment struck me as a powerful argument for letting children read as many comics as they can get their grubby little hands on. Alan, I am happy to report, still has many of those comics carefully stored away.

As to the origins of my interest in science-fiction, my father and my uncle (the noted television producer Howie Horwitz) always read the stuff. The books were lying around the house. Their covers held an early fascination for me. Having read it from an early age, when I started trying my hand at fiction, it was one genre (though by no means all) that naturally attracted me. My early efforts were very imitative, and perhaps to a certain extent some of the work still is. It would depend on the critics you talk to.

All artists borrow, consciously or unconsciously, from their predecessors.

The first science-fiction book I remember reading was the Isaac Asimov short story collection *Nine Tomorrows*. The second was the juvenile *The Space Ship Under the Apple Tree*, at age eleven. And there were many, many others. I also remember A. E. van Vogt's *The World of Null A*, when I was eleven, and setting it aside as too complex to read.

Science-fiction novels and comics were not the only major influence during his childhood. He had the natural fears of most children, and he enjoyed going to the cinema, so films, too, made their mark – and one of them more than any other:

Oh, yes, it's true that I used to fear such things as dark corners. My over-active imagination was always filling them up with childhood nasties. Interestingly, very little frightened me that I could see. So the one film that really terrified me and left me watching my bedroom window for months afterwards was one of the greatest science-fiction films of all times, MGM's 1956 production of *Forbidden Planet*. The monster in it, the 'monster from the id', is more not there than there. I feared, you understand, that which I couldn't see.

Nowadays I enjoy walking about at night, and I'm not afraid of things that go bump in the dark. One other thing I don't care for are parasites: again, because you can't see them. That's what I worry about when I'm travelling in places like south-eastern Peru or Papua New Guinea – not jaguars and snakes and army ants, all of which I'm quite fond of. Exotic and alien, you see.

In an interview he gave to *Contemporary Authors* some years ago, he amplified the reasons for these views but with the benefit of hindsight, he added:

There are a number of reasons why I write primarily (though not exclusively) science-fiction. Science-fiction is the only branch of contemporary literature that cares about and deals with what's going to happen tomorrow. It is also the only genre with absolutely no restrictions. The writer of speculative fiction can do anything, absolutely anything he or she wants. The only convention is that there are no conventions. Science-fiction doesn't attract writers; it seduces them. Total creative freedom, that's very seductive.

So what were the early signs that he was destined to become a writer? What gave him the confidence to start?

I'm not sure that I was ever that confident. It was just that writing was something that I'd always been good at. When I was in high school, all the other kids preferred multiple choice or true/false tests. I was literally the only one I knew who preferred and even enjoyed essay testing.

So we know there was something out of the ordinary right there. At university I had planned to become a lawyer, but in my senior year at the

University of California at Los Angeles [UCLA], I discovered their world-class film department. I found out that I could amass credits for watching movies. You go and watch Charlie Chaplin for four hours and they give you four credits.

At the same time, almost as a lark, I took some film and television writing courses because I'd always been good at writing and I thought they would offer a few more easy credits. They did. While other students laboured over the class assignments, I found them absurdly easy. While the others took a semester to write and refine thirty minutes of screenplay, I knocked it out in two weeks and took the rest of the time off. I can't explain this – it was just a natural ability I had, the way others are good at the high jump or working out difficult math problems.

I was also very adept at and interested in the natural sciences: anything that didn't involve too much math. Biology, zoology, and the like. Same for social studies, literature – anything that demanded a lot of reading and memory work. I was also good at public speaking, and sampled a lot of diverse subjects, everything from microbiology to fencing. I think you'll find that writers who favour science-fiction all tend to be, to a greater or lesser degree, polymaths.

They're interested in everything. You have to be, if you're going to be skilled at inventing believable alternate worlds.

I was drawing pictures of rocket ships when I was seven years old and originally thought of becoming a rocket engineer. It was very disheartening to discover early on that in order to work in that field you need a certain, shall we say, minimal grounding in more than basic math.

I was also told from a very young age that I was a good writer. My work was often selected to be read aloud in class. But as to thoughts of actually basing a career on it, it never occurred to me that such a thing existed in the real world. Nor was I encouraged, beyond generalised classroom praise, to pursue the notion. All the scholastic aptitude tests that American children are required to take in school said I should become – you guessed it – a lawyer. My practical parents pointed me in that direction, and we even had lawyers in the family. Your choice was simple: doctor or lawyer. Since I didn't much care for the sight of blood, I decided to become a doctor.

Sorry – early and old joke!

I had already been admitted to the University of Southern California Law School as well as a couple of others, but I also, again almost as a lark, applied to the graduate film school at UCLA. No one was more surprised than I was, when I was granted admission. To this day I don't know why. I imagine someone saw something in my written application. If I hadn't been admitted, I would have gone on to law school and perhaps never have become a writer.

While churning out screenplays to satisfy the requirements for my Master's degree, I thought I'd have a little fun and try my hand at prose. So I did a handful of short stories and, lo and behold, the twelfth one sold. Meanwhile, none of the screenplays were attracting any professional interest. After graduating and losing my scholastic military deferment (this was during the Vietnam War when conscription was still in force), I joined the Army Active Reserve. I figured that when I got out of my six months' active duty I'd go to law school and that would be that.

But a funny thing intervened. I had written a novel, *The Tar-Aiym Krang*, and much to my surprise, it sold on its third submission, to no less than Ballantine Books. The book incorporates some wise suggestions from the editor of the first market I submitted it to. That would be John W. Campbell, the editor of the then premier SF magazine, *Analog*. Betty Ballantine, who finally bought it, published the manuscript pretty much as it stood. Meanwhile, I'm thinking to myself, 'Well, gee, I'm one for one at this, and I'm only twenty-two.'

So I thought, why not take a serious crack at this endeavour for a year and see what happens? I kind of muddled along for five or six years doing a book a year for advances running around fifteen hundred to two thousand dollars a book. Throw in a couple of short story sales, two years writing public relations, then a part-time teaching job at Los Angeles City College, and I survived pretty well. After that, everything kind of snowballed. So I wasn't an instant success in the sense that I had a lot of money right away, but I did sell right from the start.

Alan was extremely lucky in having his first book published, for he did not have an agent at the time. However, as he said, he did have one publishing contact, one of the more important editors of American science-fiction, John W. Campbell, and he had previously published one of Alan's short stories. While he had rejected Alan's book typescript, Campbell repeatedly encouraged him in subsequent letters, finally writing, 'You know, I can't buy this book because my inventory is full for the next two years, but I think you've got a pretty good yarn here. I definitely think it's saleable.'

Encouragement is so seldom given freely to those wishing to become professional writers, but when it is given it can be doubly effective. Coming from such a luminary of the science-fiction world, it made Alan feel most encouraged. He didn't have to rely on his own judgement, but an editor's. As Alan added: 'It's like with children, you know. Oftentimes, encouragement means so much more than criticism.'

His search for a publisher followed a very orthodox sequence, one which millions of would-be authors, without publishing contacts, follow.

I got a copy of a magazine called *Writer's Digest* which suggested that I should put the typescript in a brown paper envelope together with a stamped self-addressed envelope, and submit it in that fashion. And that's exactly, perhaps naively, what I did. That's how I sold my first few stories and my first book.

As I mentioned, I started writing screen- and teleplays while at the UCLA film department, as a senior at university. That's what I wanted to do: write screenplays. Being naive, I thought, you simply write something good, and somebody buys it, and you go and make a movie. Needless to say, that's not quite how it works... Returning again to beginnings: I had been writing stories and trying to sell them for months. At the time I was (and still am) a big fan of the writings of H. P. Lovecraft. So I wrote a long pseudo-story in the style of a Lovecraftian letter and sent it to August Derleth, the founder and editor of the small American publisher Arkham House. Sometime later I get back this odd letter that says, 'Read your story and would like very much to publish it in my next issue of the *Arkham Collector*.' This was his house's semi-annual literary magazine. This sent me rushing frantically to my files as I tried to remember what 'story' I had sent him. It was something I did purely for fun, and taught me a useful lesson. Everything I had been trying to write 'to the market' was going nowhere, while something I wrote out of love and personal interest sold immediately. It was published under the title *Some Notes Concerning a Green Box* and was actually my first sale, though a story I sold to Campbell at *Analog* appeared first.

Other stories appeared in journals, until he attempted that first novel. Alan was extremely fortunate, because with a firm base of several stories actually in print, he received an advance for his first book. Not much, even by the standards of the day, but $1,500 is always welcome and was worth more, of course, in 1971. *The Tar-Aiym Krang* was published in 1972 – the first of many.

Alan's big break did not occur immediately, which is hardly surprising. It did not happen, either, when his second book, *Bloodhype*, was published a year later. But his third effort was a different matter. In fact, he had a double stroke of good fortune:

> The first break, my big break, if you will, came with the publication of my third novel, *Icerigger*, which quickly sold something like a hundred and fifty thousand copies and made the genre's bestseller list. It surprised everybody including Judy-Lynn del Ray, who was then my editor at Ballantine Books (before the division was renamed Del Ray Books). It raised my credibility as a marketable writer much faster than it did my advances, as everybody ran around trying to figure out what had gone so right. A good

deal of credit was given to the cover, by Dean Ellis. Eventually they reached the conclusion that maybe, just maybe, it was real good luck. For myself, I believe strongly in word of mouth among readers. No internet back then.

Break number two came with the opportunity to do the novelisations (book versions) of the animated *Star Trek* TV series. These became the *Star Trek Logs*. Ten in all that made my name known to a much wider audience.

Star Trek spawned a cult following of ardent fans, and is if anything more popular today in its manifold incarnations than it was when the original series was on television.

The royalty payments for 'novelisations' are, however, very low, sometimes just half a per cent of the cover price, so unless a writer is going to work on a project of the scale of *Star Wars*, or the *Alien* films, as Alan has, the chances of earning much are slim indeed.

I've done spin-offs as well as straight novelisations. For George, I did the first *Star Wars* spin-off book, *Splinter of the Mind's Eye*. An original novel but set in the *Star Wars* universe. For that

I received a higher royalty than I normally do for novelisations, because a great deal more original work was involved.

He had told me how he had struck lucky very quickly, by his own efforts, but surely, I asked, as soon as sales of his third book blossomed, he had a literary agent?

Actually, I obtained an agent on the basis of my first two book sales, before *Icerigger* appeared. I had two agencies for many years: one for media, another for print.

After I'd sold the first book, I thought it would be advantageous to get an agent, even though Betty Ballantine had already pre-bought my second. So I looked in the *Science-Fiction Writers of America Handbook*, found the agents who had the most clients within the field, and picked out the top two. One of them replied, we struck up a relationship, and she's been my agent ever since.

Every writer needs help; agents certainly help by providing the contacts, but what help did he get from his wife, JoAnn?

JoAnn gives me a great deal of help. She's even been directly responsible for a couple of stories (and was the genesis of the *Mad Amos* series). But her greatest assistance lies in providing me with the kind of support I need to be able to relax and write freely.

She does this by intercepting much of the outside world and taking care of the household as well as handling much general PR. Love and support is vital because, like so many writers, I'm not an easy person to live with. Very often, I'm not just living with my stories, but living in them. If I happen to be writing a comedy, like the recent *Jed the Dead*, then I can be a joy to be around. But if I'm working on something like *Aliens*, then my moods can reflect that. She's very tolerant and understanding.

You know, the advantages of writing are obvious to most people, but the disadvantages are not. For example, you can never be free from what you are working on at the time, and you can never call in sick (who's going to replace you on the job?).

Despite the fact that he was good at English at school, and later at university, had he felt the need to be taught the craft of writing once he had started to write novels?

Never. I never read one book on writing, nor did I take any courses beyond the screen- and teleplay writing seminars at school. I never participated in any outside conferences or sessions, or belonged to any writing groups.

I taught writing for six years at college level, and the first thing I told my students when they came to class was that I could not teach them how to write. Sentence structure, grammar, elements of basic plotting, sure – but you can't teach writing.

James Herbert

The Rats, The Fog, The Spear, The Dark, The Magic Cottage, Haunted, Creed, '48, Portent, Nobody True and more than a dozen more, with worldwide sales in excess of 40 million.

JAMES HERBERT IS the British equivalent of Stephen King. Without a doubt, these two writers produce some of today's most widely read horror novels. Curiously, both had their first books published in the same year, 1974; King with *Carrie* and Herbert with *The Rats*. Of the two authors, King is more widely known in the UK, but Herbert currently outsells him here. He is a good friend of King's, the two having met through sharing the same publisher.

When interviewing authors, I am frequently struck by their ability to imagine wholly original events and situations – writers of horror stories above all others. Those at the top of this genre possess incredible skills. Where do they get their weird and spine-chilling ideas from? Perhaps from nightmares, or unhappy childhood events; perhaps even from a sadistic streak buried deep in their subconscious minds. I doubt whether anyone, writer or reader, really knows.

Herbert's first career was in advertising, mainly because at school he had developed a flair for drawing and painting. He was also good at English. After a grammar school education he went to Hornsey College of Art, leaving at the age of twenty. The main attraction of a job in advertising was not only that it was well paid, but also that he could practise what he liked doing best, art. Six years and many campaigns later, he had been promoted to Group Head, a status then unheard of for someone of only twenty-six. Usually people attained this level in their mid-thirties or forties, but he denies that he was any kind of 'whizz-kid'.

In those early days he promoted such diverse products as Chanel, Clairol, Harp lager and Van Heusen shirts, not to mention the service of more 'Establishment' clients such as clearing banks – Barclays and Midland in particular. His experience of writing was, up to then, very limited, and involved creative copy for captions, television commercials and comic strips – scarcely the kind of experience to lead one to write some of the best horror novels.

So how and why did he turn to writing at the age of twenty-eight, having had no such inclination before?

> Ego. Sheer ego. I had been very successful in advertising. I'd reached a pinnacle, and I told myself I could do anything. Yes, sure, there was always better work that you can do in advertising, and better positions, but it wasn't fulfilling me. I began looking for a new challenge.
>
> That's post-rationale, looking back, but it may not have been true at the time, you understand? I was very successful and I had been promoted at a very early stage – so I thought, what else is there to do? And I thought about writing books. Also, I had so much energy at the time, I needed another outlet that was both creative and challenging.
>
> It all sounds very glib now, but it seemed a good idea at the time.

These sounded like the views of a very ambitious man, but what became clear was that his role as a Group Head took him away from what he liked doing best, using his skills as an artist and creative copy writer.

Did he make a clean break from advertising, or try, like other hopeful authors, to start writing in his spare moments?

> Oh yes. It was just evenings and weekends, which was crazy, because in advertising, it's pretty hairy. You often have to work into the evenings and at weekends as well. It was difficult, but I wrote in any free moment I had, which was bad news for my wife and daughters.
>
> Writing increased the pressure, you know. It certainly wasn't an antidote to pressures of work in advertising.
>
> I also opened a colour laboratory at the same time and I was there in the studio, painting, putting up partitions and arranging cameras. I loved it, but both distracted me from advertising. One failed, the colour lab, thank God!

But where, I asked, did he get the ideas for his first book, *The Rats*?

> Oh, way back. I lived in the East End of London, which was like five hundred yards from the City of London. Whitechapel and Aldgate were the

scummy side of London. The part of London which you'd never wish to live in.

When I was a kid, I used to have a scooter; later, I bought a bike for ten bob [50p] in Brick Lane, and I used to escape and cycle, or scoot, all around the City which, on a Saturday or Sunday morning, would always be deserted; the whole atmosphere of those lovely buildings, always empty... Not slums, you understand, just open and free of people. It was a pervasive image that I have recreated in many of my novels.

Many of my childhood ideas are milling somewhere around in my memory. When I sit down to write they surface again.

There's a lot of truth in all the books I've written. In every one, there's something that's affected me, the good things and the bad.

That is why in *The Rats*, I had London empty and, in *The Fog*, London gone berserk.

Childhood memories of places and sights remain with us for the rest of our lives. Herbert still vividly recalls the devastation of the bomb-sites left over from the last war, places where children used to play during the day, and rats at night. There were still a good many bomb-sites and at night, unlit, they presented a stark and forbidding background (again, recalled in Herbert's eighteenth novel, '48).

He also remembered seeing Bela Lugosi as Dracula. In one scene, thousands of rats appear, and their myriad eyes appeared to stare out at him as he watched. At this point Jim (as he likes to be called) echoed the advice of so many other writers: 'You're supposed to write about something you know, so it seemed an obvious choice. I was very familiar with the scary sight of rats scampering around in the East End, so why not write about them?'

When the manuscript of *The Rats* was finished, he sent copies out to six different publishers at the same time. Hardly adhering to convention – many publishers still frown on 'multiple submissions', especially from first-time authors – but as he had no contacts in the book publishing world, it seemed to him a logical thing to do. To me this is a sign of an eager author determined to get someone to publish his work. What happened to the typescripts, and who gave him the break, I asked?

Well, one went to Gollancz and one to Michael Joseph. Both turned me down. Eventually New

English Library accepted it and we went on from there. The other three also rejected it, even though they knew NEL was interested. One, at least, hadn't even bothered to read the manuscript.

Having taken him on, New English Library only paid Herbert £150 as an advance against future royalties – he probably earns that tenfold each day now. Being in advertising, and having written copy for countless advertisements, he was used to seeing his words in print. Perhaps he was less excited than other first-time writers when the book came out?

Oh no. In the first place, I was ecstatic when I received a letter saying that it was going to be published.

Then I got a great kick like every other author when it was finally published, but I was soon brought down to earth. I remember it well. They published on a Thursday. And I went into W. H. Smith in Cheapside, where, over the years, because my agency was nearby, I frequently bought books. Sometimes I bought three, four or five at a time. Sometimes I think I kept them going!

I went in and looked for *The Rats* in hardback, and didn't see it anywhere. I mean, that's how naive I was. I expected to see it. I saw the manageress and said, 'Um, have you got a book, called *The Rats* from New English Library?' I was too embarrassed to say my own name: 'by James Herbert'.

She said, 'No. And we are not likely to have that sort of book.'

That was a choker for me. On my big day, too. But it was a good lesson to learn, though it did spoil the day for me.

It was not unreasonable for Jim to expect to see a few copies. After all, New English Library had an initial print run of 100,000 copies, a huge order suggesting that mass circulation was planned. The publishers ran out of stock after three weeks, and since then there have been at least thirty-three reprints.

Then came the reviews, or so Jim hoped. The following weekend found him rushing down to his local newsagents to buy all the 'Sundays'. There was absolutely nothing in any of them. This put a further dampener on the heady joys of becoming an author – as it does for so many other writers. Then *The*

Observer finally published a review. It was terrible, and condensed, ran: 'this is rubbish, deserves to be tossed into the dustbin.'

> I said to my wife, Eileen, 'Well, it's obvious I'm not a writer.' I mean I was truly crushed. You spend a year working evenings and weekends, doing something you really believe in. And you've got to remember that *The Rats* wasn't just a horror story for me, it was a comment on the East End as I knew it; the way it had been neglected by governments over the years since the war. I was really incensed. How could they say it was rubbish? I was ready to give it all up, and I nearly did.
>
> The very next weekend, *The Sunday Times* carried a very different review. They said it was brilliant. My confidence was immediately restored. So I learned the lesson that everybody is entitled to their views...
>
> In the end, I realised that you can't listen to anybody. It was neither brilliant nor rubbish.

After *The Rats*, was he commissioned by his publishers to write another?

Yes, they asked me to do another book, and I wouldn't accept it. I wouldn't be commissioned.

It's a very funny story. I did *The Rats*, then they said, 'Can we have all your other manuscripts? We would be interested in anything you've written before.' I said, 'No. No. I promise you that is it.' They tried again, and said they would like to commission me.

But I said, 'No, I'm in advertising. I've got a great job and it's good money. I don't know whether the book was a flash in the pan or not. I don't even know if I can write another one.' I said I would certainly try. 'I enjoy the process. If I manage to write another, then we can talk.'

So I wrote *The Fog* and they took me out to lunch. They actually tried to get me drunk, so that I would say, yes, OK, they can have it, but that's a very bad mistake to make with me. Within forty-five minutes the editor was literally under the table. He kept popping his head up and repeating, 'Jim, I shink you shud come with ush...' I said, 'No way.' It was very funny, really. Very, very few can out-drink me!

At that time, I didn't know much about publishing, and I figured the publishers had a good deal with the first one. I decided to get an agent and find out a bit more about the business, and what they should be paying. That's what I did in the end.

It was an innocent event at work that gave Herbert the idea for *The Fog*. He was in his office, and sitting at his desk, when a rather boring visitor got up and walked over to the open window. Jim's mind began to wander a little. What if he were to jump out, he thought? What if the population of London began to jump out of windows? What could make them do it? A poisonous gas, perhaps? From these fleeting moments of imagination sprang the concept for *The Fog*.

I had read this book, and when I commented on it, he exclaimed, with some feeling, that all interviewers who came to see him had only read *The Fog* or *The Rats*, though he had written many other and better books. He felt that I should read *The Magic Cottage*. When, later, I did so, I found it an equally good read though totally different. I was also struck by the design and presentation of the book and its jacket, but then I should have been – Jim was the designer. The jacket had great visual appeal, the endpapers were decorated, and the text was illustrated; he even chose the typeface. Few authors are lucky enough to be able to design their own books.

After the success of each of his novels, had he ever considered what it was that made them so popular? Did he believe, for example, that he was writing novels that the public wanted, or was he writing to suit himself?

I used to say in interviews that I just happened to tune in to public taste; what they wanted at the time. Then I realised, looking more deeply into it, that I didn't tune in to anybody, but the public tuned in to me. There were lots of horror writers around, but none had made the big breakthrough. I – and Stephen King – happened to offer something different, in the way that Presley, and then The Beatles, did in music.

To an extent, my personality shows in my writing. Mine comes through in the humour. That's more me than the supernatural, though there's obviously some corner in my mind that drags out all this horror and the bizarre. I'm not going to say nastiness, because that's a label I despise.

It's directed towards that certain aspect, of life and death, if you like. That comes out, but there is a lot of humour in the idealism. Call me a cynical idealist, because there's a lot of cynicism in my books, but always, in the end, they're optimistic. They always have that bit of hope at the end. And again, that's in my nature.

And I know that the public's taste varies over the years. A lot of kids write to me to say they loved *The Rats*, loved it, the blood and the gore, but I'm not into that any more. If it happens in a story that there is a piece of blood and a piece of ghoul, then fine, but I'm not writing solely for that. I know that a few other horror writers are out to exploit that, but I like to be moving on.

Each of my books is little different from the others and I carry most of my old readers with me and collect new ones on the way. I think, for my sake, I have to do something different each time. If you read *The Magic Cottage*, and then read *Sepulchre*, you'd think that they were written by two different people, and then if you read *Haunted*, you'd think that they were by three different authors. *Fluke* isn't even a horror story.

But there are certain people who write the same thing time and time again. That's fine, if they want to do it, and the readers still buy it, [but] eventually the public will find you out, and ultimately reject your work. I also think you're damaging your own creative ability by writing to format.

So, if Herbert varies the books each time, how does he assess the importance of the ingredients: the plot, characters, subject, and storyline?

If you tried to pin it down to the ingredients, I don't think the separate ingredients are the answer. You can't say, because they're devious, because they're sexy, because they're humorous, or because they have a *grande* theme, they will be successful. It's just the way the story is told, which is why I say that there is something indefinable, a kind of magic, about putting words on to paper.

Every ingredient you mention is important, but it is the alchemy that brings it all together. You can't just define it, because if you could, then everyone would be doing it. If everybody knew the secret, there would be several thousand bestselling authors.

It doesn't have to be high literature, but it has to be literate. And you have to tell a good story.

And I will write a sex scene if it's called for. If the story warrants a sex scene, I'll usually write it in detail. If one can write about horror in detail, why should I not write about sex in detail? And sex is a wonderful thing to describe, but it has got to be of value to the story. It sounds a cliché, but it's true.

Given his unusual break into writing, I wondered whether his advice to would-be writers would be significantly different from that of other successful authors.

In the first place, it's no good asking for advice and just talking about it [i.e. writing a book]! You've just got to sit down and endure... But there are practical things.

I always tell them to get *The Writers' and Artists' Yearbook*, just so that they can see how to set out a manuscript.

Research your subject, and jot down one line ideas. And always plan your book.

James A. Michener

I write about just what I want to write about. Supposing, some years ago, you had gathered together all the bright people in publishing and said to them that you wanted to bring out a book that will knock them dead; that will stay at the top of the bestseller list for over a year; and that everybody will want to get a copy of?

Do you think that the group would have said, what the world really yearns for is a book about an archeological dig in the Holy Land? Going back five thousand years? No way. No way.

Or, a few years later, about a rabbit travelling through the north of England?

No, books are written by writers. And writers are people with insights and imagination. With courage and crazy ideas, and some of them pay off.

You know, you write your first three books at four o'clock in the morning, and you have a full day's job. Then you want a little exercise, or a little recreation. Go to bed early, and that alarm goes again at four. You'd better get up again. If you can't, I don't think you'll make it.

It can also be at eleven o'clock at night, but

there has to be a time for you to prosecute your dream, while you're doing something else to live.

And the bulk of us do that, and if that terrifies you, or you feel you don't have the sticking quality, or if your wife can't visualise the long apprenticeship, then don't start.

Unless you wear bifocals by the age of twenty-two, you'll never make it. You haven't read enough. I don't know how you get a feeling of what a great book is, or what fine people have done in your generation, unless you read something. I don't think it can be done by osmosis. So maybe I'm stressing my own education too strongly, but I still believe it.

...ays write from the heart.
- Strong central character
- Sub-plot?

THINGS TO CONSIDER
• Finding an agent
• Overcoming writer's block
... writer should always
... a notebook & pen.

Part 2

Sagas and romance

Barbara Taylor Bradford

A Woman of Substance, Voice of The Heart,
To Be The Best, Dangerous To Know, Love
In Another Town, A Secret Affair, Her Own
Rules, Power of A Woman, Just Rewards,
Unexpected Blessings and Emma's Secret.
Over 75 million copies sold worldwide.

SOMEONE ONCE ASKED me what a novel is and I said, 'It's a monumental lie that has to have the absolute ring of truth if it is to succeed.' So Barbara Taylor Bradford wrote in a feature article aptly titled, 'So You Want to Write a Bestseller?'

This pearl of wisdom, reiterated at our meeting, first appeared in the 1988 edition of the *American Writer's Handbook*, and she was well qualified to make it, having published eight bestselling novels by then. In one week, as long ago as June 1986, she had two of her titles at the top of the UK's bestselling lists at the same time: *Act of Will* in the hardback list and *Hold That Dream* in the paperback. With these and two other novels, her total sales of just the English language editions were reported in late 1989 to have exceeded 30 million copies. Today, her books have been translated in over 40 languages.

People from Yorkshire are known for their bluntness and for their single-mindedness in pursuing what they seek. The origin of Barbara's confident directness and determination can be traced to her early life. Her upbringing must take much of the credit; it is a period which is still very clear in her mind today, as she wrote in her article in the *Writer's Handbook*:

> When I was ten, my father bought me a second-hand typewriter and I typed out these little tales and stitched them in a folder with a hand-painted title.
>
> When I was twelve I submitted one – about a little horse, I think – to something called *The Children's Magazine* and it was actually published.

She got seven-and-sixpence. That was a lot of pocket money to a small child in 1945, and it certainly made a big impression on her. It was, too, the first time she saw her name in print, which added to the impact. Put the two together and one can understand why Barbara, with the benefit of hindsight, proclaims, 'My destiny was sealed that day I saw my name in print.'

Unlike many other writers, her emergence as an author of bestselling fiction was no 'second-career decision', but a conscious ambition from a very early age. Her mother, Freda, a former children's nurse and nanny, was an insatiable reader, and introduced Barbara to books when she was four. By the time she was twelve she had read all of Dickens's novels and those of the Brontë sisters (not, she admits, that she fully understood them all). Once hooked on the habit, she read avidly at all hours, even by torchlight under the bedclothes at night.

Her mother supported Barbara in other ways, too. For example, she introduced her to classical music and ballet at the Theatre Royal in Leeds, and encouraged her to believe that, provided she worked hard enough, she could achieve anything she wanted. Barbara is full of admiration and gratitude for her parents' help, to which she owes so much. Although naturally gifted, she has always been very ready to acknowledge their support, saying of her mother:

> She really did make me feel rather special. And
> I do believe the whole thing of Freud's, which is
> 'give me the child till the age of seven, and I will
> give you the man, or woman.'

Barbara attended Christ Church Elementary School and then Northcote Private School for Girls in Leeds, where she studied shorthand and typing. She excelled at English literature, however, and in this respect she shares a common link with other authors like Dora Saint and Penny Jordan, or Craig Thomas and Frederick Forsyth. She was awarded several certificates for her English, and this doubtless helped get her first job with the *Yorkshire Evening Post* in 1948.

Her meteoric rise to bestsellerdom has been recounted many times, but these articles or programmes usually follow the basic details from the biographical notes handed out by her publicists. These are necessarily brief, and omit the background that lies behind the bland statements of success. In particular, they usually leave out the events that led up to an author's break into writing.

Although she had always dreamed of becoming a writer from childhood, it was when she became a cub reporter that her life really changed. This, as her millions of fans will know, began with her local paper, the *Yorkshire Evening Post*, as she told me:

I started work at my local paper's office as a junior typist, typing letters for the advertising people. I used to make lots of mistakes on their expensive stationery, and my pile of waste daily grew steadily higher, so out of embarrassment I took some waste sheets into the ladies' room and set fire to them over the toilet, but I took much more home to burn in my mother's grate. I always had problems reading my shorthand book. This went on for weeks, but towards the end of the first three months, the lady who ran the typing pool put me in the telephonists' room.

There, you sat at a little desk with earphones on, and a typewriter in front of you. Whenever a reporter phoned in saying 'I want to dictate a story...' you began typing. One of those reporters was Keith Waterhouse and I remember he once phoned to dictate a story and it went, 'Today, a fire broke out in the Queen's Hotel and nine people were killed...' [The story was big news at the time and she and Waterhouse became great friends afterwards. Years later, he went on to become famous in his own right, as a novelist – he wrote *Billy Liar*, among others – journalist and playwright. At the time, they both realised that of all those they knew at the newspaper, they were the only two determined to get on in life.]

With a cup of machine-made coffee in my hand, I regularly used to take this sort of thing down to the sub-editors' room. This was a big room with desks and people everywhere. Some got to know me, and it was there that I met a reporter, Arthur Brittenden, but he worked for the *Yorkshire Post*. I made it known to him, and to another girl who also worked for the *Yorkshire Post* and who had become a great friend of mine, Jean Stead, that I wanted to become a reporter. She said, 'The only way you'll become a reporter is to move out of the typing pool and start writing things.' 'For the *Yorkshire Post* or *Evening Post*?' I asked. '*The Evening Post*, of course. Maybe you could do a little feature or something.'

Then I quite coincidentally stumbled onto one. There was an old woman who lived in Armley, and I remember, as a child, that everyone called her 'the old witch'. Polly was just like the old woman who lived in a shoe, except that she didn't have any children. She was very poor, and a sort of menace in many ways; she had all these cats and dogs, and would often wave her stick at everybody passing. People were always complaining about 'Old Polly'.

Well, it turned out that she was the sister of one of the wealthiest men in Leeds. My story was about Polly Legard, or 'Old Polly', the woman who lived in a shoe but had a brother who owned all these buses... and Jean helped me put it together. I quickly learnt how long a piece should be, and when I had finished it, I just dumped it anonymously on a sub-editor's desk, a usual thing for me to do, and it got printed as a little feature.

I kept on doing little features like this, and dumping them on the subs' desks. They usually got published.

Like any workaholic, she was known to stay on late at work, writing something, anything, just to get it in the paper. For Barbara, getting published was a case of hard work and Yorkshire grit.

Then one day I was sitting typing letters and looking at my shorthand book, wondering, as usual, what a squiggle was, when the lady who ran the pool, an ogre by the name of Miss Worfolk, came up to me and said accusingly, 'What have you done? The editor wants to see you.'

At sixteen, I was still a little fearless; anyway, I knew who the editor was, and off I went. But it was very unusual for the editor to ask to see a junior.

Outside his office, his secretary gave me an odd look, a bit of a scowl, and said, 'Go in.' And into the inner sanctum I went. Barry Horniblow worked in a very large and imposing room. There he sat, behind his large desk. 'Sit down,' he said – it was more of a command really – so I did, facing him, full of awe, across his desk. What had I done? What had I done? Our conversation went something like this:

'So you're Barbara Taylor.'

'Yes.'

'Are you the Barbara Taylor who wrote these stories?' he asked, as he brought out a bunch of press clippings. Four little things they were, [each] seven hundred words or so, written over a period of two months.

'Yes, why? They must have been alright, as they were published.'

I was nervous, so much so that I managed to lose my shoe under the desk. He went on unaware of my predicament.

'Well, we have to pay you. When the accounts tried to pay Barbara Taylor, they thought it was a stringer from somewhere in Knaresborough or Doncaster. No one could find a person of that name. Eventually, they found that it was you here in the typing pool.'

'Oh sir,' I said, 'you want to pay me? Is that what you wanted me for?'

'Yes. But tell me, why did you write these pieces? Do you want to be a reporter, then?'

'Oh, I don't want to be, sir. I'm going to be,' was my reply. Talk about fools rushing in where angels fear to tread!

'Did you write them all yourself?' he asked.

'Yes, well, Jean showed me a little bit.'

'Jean who?'

'Jean Stead.'

'And how do you know her?'

'Well, she sometimes lets me go with her on Saturdays,' He laughed at this. 'You do the leg work for someone on the *Yorkshire Post*?'

But I didn't mind, as I was learning. Then I told him, flushed with enthusiasm, that I had done other pieces for the local papers. 'Do you keep clippings?'

'Oh yes,' I replied, 'I've got a clippings book.'

'Well, sometime, let me see them, and we'll see what we can do.'

I left his office, returned to the pool and finished the letter. But instead of going to the canteen for lunch, I set off home to get the clippings book. I took the tram back to Upper Armley. My mother was very surprised to see me; she thought I'd been given the sack, and was quick to say so. She was praying for me to get the sack because then I could go back to my schooling and, later, on to Leeds University to finish my education. I grabbed my clippings book, ran all the way back up the street and just caught the tram back. I made it to the office, I think, within the allotted hour off for lunch, but it was very close!

There was no one outside Mr Horniblow's office. His secretary must have gone for lunch, so I knocked, and on hearing the phone being put down, entered.

'I've got my clippings book,' I said.

'But how did you get that? You didn't have it at ten o'clock this morning.' I told him how I had rushed home. 'Had any lunch? No? Well, come in and sit down.' He picked up the phone and asked his secretary, who had by then returned from lunch, for a sandwich for me and one for him, and a glass of milk. He was very sweet. He talked to me and we ate our sandwiches together and from that moment on, she hated me.

I gave him the clippings, glued in a school exercise book, and told him that they were mostly from the *Armley and Wortley News*. He must have been impressed, for after a long silence he said, 'When we get a new women's page editor, I'll probably move you into the reporters' room. Until then, keep writing.'

Three months later, I moved.

Barry Horniblow thereafter became more than an editor, more even just an employer; he became her hero, someone to emulate. When he left for a job in Fleet Street, joining the *Daily Sketch*, he set a goal for her: to work as a journalist in London's Fleet Street.

Most accounts of how authors broke into writing are glossed over in a few sentences; certainly they don't compare to Barbara's own recollection. Nor do they give any aspirant author a chance to discover what it is that singles one writer out for fame and fortune, yet not others.

Was Barbara just plain lucky, or did she engineer her good fortune? And if she did engineer it, was it through brazen confidence that she would do what she wanted to do?

Perhaps her friendships with Jean Stead and Keith Waterhouse helped shape her career more than she realised at the time, but life was not always easy. She achieved her first ambition by starting work as a cub reporter in the newsroom. It was an environment in which she learned all about society's problems: the rich pattern of daily-enacted dramas; the coroner's courts, the crimes committed, and the problems the local police encountered. Above all, she witnessed the emotions of the people involved in all these events. Any reporter will testify that the pressures of working in a newsroom can be horrific.

To Barbara, working as a reporter on a newspaper was only a step along the path of her ambition to be a writer. Certainly the number of successful authors who started in journalism suggests that it is an excellent beginning. The wide range of subject matter, and the discipline required, provide not only the confidence to write, but also that other vital ingredient, experience.

However, once assigned to the promised post on the women's page, more genteel subjects became the order of the day, such as trends in fashion, or local social events. The pages editor, Madeline McCloughlin, invited Barbara to go with her on a special trip to Paris for a major fashion show.

The trip encouraged Barbara to start what she thought was to be her first full-length novel, about an unhappy Parisian ballet dancer, Vivienne Ramage, who lived in great poverty. The story was to be full of drama, but she had scarcely started writing when she stopped, thinking that the plot reminded her of another book, *La Dame aux Camélias* by Alexandre Dumas *fils*.

> I thought, I've read that before. Somewhere. I can't do that. And that is where it ended. And that reminds me, years later, when I was writing about Emma Harte as a child in *A Woman of Substance*, I had this marvellous line – 'the strongest steel goes through the hottest fire' – two days later, I remembered it came from David Copperfield.

She struck out the line, as she abandoned her first 'novel'. All of which does show how easy it is to retain in the memory passages read over the years, and thus innocently to plagiarise another writer's work.

Back at the *Yorkshire Evening Post*, exceedingly hard work and a certain amount of luck brought dividends. She became, aged only eighteen, the editor of their women's page. Two years later, an opportunity occurred to join *Woman's Own* in London. It was an exciting move, for not only did it mean leaving home, it meant that she would be much nearer the world of the Fleet Street newspapers. As the fashion editor, she had to concentrate on publishing requirements, and she gave little indication of the world-beating novelist lying dormant within her. Once in London, Barbara was tempted by other work. After a year at *Woman's Own* she joined the *London Evening News* as a feature writer, then became a feature writer on *Today* magazine, and was for a time an executive editor of the *London American*.

Naturally, her work brought her into contact with many successful and self-motivated people – businessmen, actors, film stars and, of course, politicians – characters whose experiences and emotions would be stored away in her mind for future novels. She little suspected that she was herself destined to marry a Hollywood movie producer, or that she would reach the pinnacle of fame as a self-motivated achiever in her own right.

In 1963 she married Robert Bradford, and moved to the States. One could easily imagine that, having attained so much in such a short career, and with the advantages of being the wife of a successful film producer, she would now relax and enjoy married life. The fact that she continued her career, first in journalism, then as a compiler and editor of books, demonstrates just how much determination the would-be novelist needs.

After a while Barbara returned to her literary work in earnest. Her first edited book was for the young, *Children's Stories of the Bible from the Old Testament*. It was relatively easy for her, given her background and experience, to write publishable material. From a publisher's standpoint, she was already an established writer, editor and journalist; a far cry from all those people struggling to become writers while working at other jobs.

Her new lifestyle doubtless gave her ideas, and she set about writing what became *The Complete Encyclopedia of Homemaking Ideas*, which was published by Meredith Press in 1968. The choice of subject, publication and promotion were all well timed and sales took off, but it was not a book likely to catch the eyes of fiction reviewers. Three years – and two other titles later – she produced a second 'homemaking' book, *Easy Steps To Successful Decorating*. This sold over 165,000 copies – a bestseller for sure, though not one for which she is remembered.

For the vast majority of authors, sales of this magnitude would be fulfilling enough. They would, too, suggest that the writer had found a niche, and few would be tempted to change direction and turn to fiction. The book attracted the attention of *Newsday*'s syndication department, who asked her to write a regular column for them. She readily agreed and, under the by-line 'Designing Woman', wrote three articles a week which appeared initially in eighty to a hundred newspapers. Barbara added, 'After I had been doing it for twelve years, it appeared in 183 papers across America! That's quite a number and a major achievement.'

While all this was going on, she still hankered to become a novelist. She admits to starting four books which she never managed to finish.

I don't know why I stopped. I think I was in the wrong genre. They were more the Helen MacInnes suspense-type of thrillers. In fact, the last one I started reached one-hundred-and-twenty-five pages... [But] one Monday morning, I suddenly stopped. I looked at it and thought, this is another one I'm bored with. If I'm bored with it, then the reader will be bored.

I sat there, and I literally asked myself a lot of questions. I've got to decide why I keep starting a novel and getting so far. Some were three-hundred pages long. What's wrong? I asked myself, what do I really want to write about?

These semi-suspense novels weren't working for me. My God, what do you want to write about, Barbara? I thought, I'm nearly forty. If I don't do it now, I never will.

I thought long and hard. In the end, I decided that I wanted to write a saga, perhaps a family saga, but certainly a saga. I wanted to write about England, more specifically, Yorkshire. I wanted it to be one of those long, traditional, old-fashioned novels, about a woman who makes it in a man's world, at a time when women weren't expected to do that. I wanted to write about a woman of substance... I wrote that down in longhand, and that's how my first real novel started. And the phrase stuck too, becoming the title.

I never set out to write a bestseller, and make lots of money. I just wanted to tell this story and

> I think that's why the books work. They come
> from the heart, not from the head.

Perhaps it was her homesickness for Yorkshire that sparked it all off. Anyone who has suffered it knows just how strong this yearning can become, and how unsettling, too. Unconsciously, Barbara had discovered the missing ingredient: as her readers know, expressing emotions is one of her writing strengths.

Once her idea was on paper, she realised that she did not know what Leeds was like in 1904, nor all sorts of other historical details. So she flew to England to research the facts, to view the setting, and to interview her relatives, at the same time assuaging her homesickness. Armed with the information she needed, she finished the book in just eighteen months.

When *A Woman of Substance* was published in the USA in 1979 (and 1980 in the UK), it hit the jackpot. It became an instant bestseller, running far ahead of any of her dreams; when the first paperback edition went to press, the first print-run reached 1.4 million copies. Sales reached 3.5 million in the first year of publication. To most of her readers, and to the media, for that matter, this was her first successful book. It is certainly the one most talked about. Yet she had had ten books published before *A Woman of Substance* saw the light of day, none of which bore any similarity to this first novel.

A Woman of Substance did not get the major hype treatment, as is the case with so many authors' first novels. Nevertheless, the book made the bestseller lists for several weeks, reaching number seven in the *New York Times*. She feels very strongly that it was the book itself that made her success, rather than any publicity or hype.

The storyline centres on a strong-minded Yorkshire woman, Emma Harte, who is determined to become a successful business leader. But before she can achieve her ambition she has to confront and overcome many personal handicaps – from a humble start in life, inadequate education, to the customs and prejudices of the day. This sounds a little like Barbara Cartland, except that Cartland concentrates on the aristocracy and on virginal heroines, whereas Barbara Taylor Bradford's heroines seek material power, success, and a release from poverty. This would seem to emphasise authors' frequent advice to would-be writers: write what you know about.

Sales really accelerated when Avon Books brought out the paperback edition. They promoted *A Woman of Substance* in magazines, and produced a television commercial which appeared during popular talk shows. To all this was added that other ingredient, the personal recommendation. Word soon spread, and the result was huge sales. This book alone has sold over 20 million copies.

Writers of Barbara's standing can command unbelievably large advances. She was paid something 'in the region of ten million dollars' for her next three titles. I was still absorbing this when she added:

It was actually more than that, when you consider this was for US and Canadian hardback and paperback rights only.

Evidently, to reach this level of success you have to be more than just a talented writer. An acute business mind helps too.

The only books about writing that she has read were borrowed from the local library, but this was early on in her career, when she was training to become a journalist.

Barbara believes that there is no one who can teach you to become a novelist, but she is ready to pass on some tips:

Basic writing ability is still not enough. A would-be novelist must also observe what I call the five 'Ds'.

D for desire – the desire to want to write that novel more than do anything else.

D for drive – the drive to get started.

D for determination – the will to continue whatever the stumbling blocks and difficulties encountered on the way.

D for discipline – the discipline to write every day, whatever your mood.

D for dedication to the project until the very last page is finished.

Finally, there is a sixth D – to avoid! This is for distractions – perhaps the most important D of all, the enemy of all writers, whether would-be or proven.

Barbara Cartland

I cut everything, and my paragraphs are very short, not more than two to four lines if possible. So it's awfully easy to read.

I was asked if I thought anybody could write a book and have it published. I can't remember what it was, but I think it was called *Wings of Love*. I finished it, and sent it in under a false name, and with false details about myself, to a publisher [name deleted to spare their blushes]. They returned the manuscript, saying that I ought to go on writing and perhaps I would have a chance in the future. I then changed the author's name back to mine, and sent it to my usual publisher, and it sold enormously well, like all the others.

It just goes to show that the whole thing is hocus-pocus.

People write to me all the time, asking for advice; how they ought to paragraph and so on. They have long lumping paragraphs and they obviously don't take the trouble. They are frightfully casual about it all.

I'm terribly fussy and send things in beautifully typed and beautifully done. Everything must be in absolutely perfect order.

Penny Jordan

Falcon's Prey, Now or Never, Mistress to Her Husband, Bedding His Virgin Mistress and over 150 other titles. Worldwide sales 86 million.

MENTIONING THE BRITISH publishers Mills and Boon, will usually – like mentioning Barbara Cartland – guarantee an immediate reaction. Opinions amongst women seem to be divided between one of smug cynicism that states that such novels are trash or pap, and its opposite, which say they 'make a very good read'. Most people will admit to having read a Harlequin Mills and Boon title at some time or other, though few, I have found, enthuse wildly about them. Nevertheless, the publishers are very successful.

This is the one publisher whose name epitomises romance. Since it was founded in 1908, this unusual publishing company has carved a unique place for itself in literary history. Today the company of Harlequin Mills and Boon, part of Harlequin Enterprises, claims to sell over 200 million books a year. The imprint of Mills and Boon has become a cult name among readers of romantic novels.

Unlike writers published by other companies mentioned in this book, Mills and Boon authors rarely get the same degree of high-profile publicity as that enjoyed by, say, Barbara Taylor Bradford. A few have been promoted, people like Sally Beauman, Charlotte Lamb, Anne Weale, Marjorie Lewty, Elizabeth Power and Dana James, but most authors who contribute to M and B's output are relatively unknown. Many prefer it that way. In all, the company averages some thirty-two novels a month, which at least suggests that there is scope for new authors.

Penny Jordan, one of Mills and Boon's more successful authors, is certainly one who eschews publicity. The publisher's press release provided me with some background notes about her, but I was amazed to discover that she had actually published over one hundred books. It seems clear that, where Mills and Boon romances are concerned, it is the publisher's imprint that is important, rather than the individual author.

Penny, as I have said, avoids publicity, but this does not seem to have affected her sales.

I've done the odd newspaper interview and a few radio discussions. But I'm terribly anti all publicity. I know it sells books, and I know it's the new way, but I still hate it.

Her home in Cheshire is set high on a hill with impressive views of the surrounding countryside, although it is only a few miles from Macclesfield. The fourteenth century Yeoman's Hall in which she lives is full of oak beams and panelling, and during our discussion we sat in a room so furnished, her office-cum-library.

It is possible that Penny Jordan personifies the ideal image of the romantic writer.

I didn't specifically want a career. Girls in my day didn't normally have careers, they normally worked until they got married, then left and had a family.

When Steve and I got married, we decided, for financial reasons, that both of us would need to continue working. Until then, I hadn't thought I would have to, and I had no intentions of having a working career.

My schooldays were nothing exceptional. I went to a small grammar school and managed to get three O-levels; I don't know how I achieved that miracle. Then my parents sent me to a secretarial college in Wortham, which is near Manchester, because I don't think they knew what to do with me. From there I went to work, for short spells, at the London and Lancashire Insurance Company, two small firms of solicitors, and then at the Midland Bank.

I enjoyed working at the bank very much, mainly because I was working for a manager, and dealing with people. I was there quite a long time so I got to know most of the customers quite well. It was all very personal then, but we still kept records. We would see their whole lives developing, with all their ups and downs. It was all very interesting, but nowadays it's become quite mechanized, or so I've heard from friends. Without that personal touch you had with the customer, it isn't as interesting as it was. People tell you that banking is boring. It isn't boring at all, nothing dealing with people is ever boring.

I actually started writing when I was thirty, so for a long time I wrote and worked.

Here, then, is another who began her writing career while working full-time in another occupation. It seems such an obvious way to begin, but not all authors agree. Penny started writing in 1976, but it was some time before she had anything published.

> I always wanted to write and I thought when I was thirty, if you are going to do anything with your life, now is the time.
>
> There wasn't a specific reason. Steve was working hard, and we'd moved house and did not go out very much, so I had lots of time on my hands which I wanted to fill.
>
> I was a great starter, but not a finisher, and my thanks go to Steve and one particular brother-in-law, both keen readers like me, who thought it would be of value if I could actually manage to finish something.
>
> You spend a lot of time thinking, well, I'll do that one day, I'll do that another day, and suddenly when you're thirty you think...

She paused for a moment.

> You know, I didn't specifically think I could do it, but it was the achievement of actually sitting down and writing something, and finishing it. That was the achievement. That was the goal,

and it seemed very, very, grown-up to sit down and actually finish something.

And that gave me a degree of confidence, but I didn't feel really confident until I had a book out.

She paused again, and our conversation returned to her school days. Penny disclosed that one of her problems at school had been that, though she naturally wrote left-handed, she was often forced to do so right-handed. Perhaps this pressure affected her results – clearly, she was no scholar, though she did excel at English. Even then, however, she did not enjoy the set writing.

You always had to write to order. You'd be given a subject, and they were never subjects that I wanted to write about.

It wasn't until I actually sat down and started using my imagination, instead of daydreaming, that it really all started to flow. And I did day-dream a lot, especially through French lessons, about the stories I had read in books, and continuations of them.

Penny graduated into writing through her own efforts. She joined a local writers' group, where the varied subjects tackled stimulated her interest, though not many of those attending the course were writing fiction. But, like Clive Cussler, she did seek advice from a writing school.

> I paid for the course, but it really was a waste of both time and money. I knew that my dialogue wasn't right, it didn't flow easily and the whole thing was stilted. I actually thought, maybe a writing school would help me polish up on that, but in reality it didn't. It was so basic. It was less helpful than what I knew by instinct, which wasn't an awful lot. So, you know, I agree with the majority. I don't believe those courses can teach you to write. I think it's simply commonsense.

Why had she chosen romance for her fiction?

> Ah well, I love romance. Especially historical romance. I don't like everything, there has to be a happy ending, though.
> I like Barbara Taylor Bradford's books and I liked Georgette Heyer, so when I started, I had a try at that sort of thing. Not specifically trying

to copy her work, but you tend to write what you admire.

Eventually it came over me that it would be really nice to have something published, and of course, by this time I had read enough, and knew enough, to know that it's very difficult for an unknown writer, especially for someone like myself. And I'd read somewhere, a women's magazine I think, that Mills and Boon were always looking for new writers. I had read a lot of their books and I thought, why don't I try?

Then followed a long period of time when I wrote three words, three lines, or three chapters. You know, for months, perhaps, I wouldn't touch the typewriter, then I would stay up all hours of the night writing. Sometimes, the idea would dry up and it would be thrown away, or put into the drawer. Eventually I got something finished and I sent it off to them.

They had it for about three months, and I thought to myself, that's a waste of paper again. It was between Christmas and the New Year and I must have had a sudden surge of decision-making, so I telephoned them, and a voice said, 'Oh yes, we've just written to you about it, and we'd like to publish it, but it needs a few alterations.'

I nearly fell out of my chair. I couldn't believe it. I would have liked to have written historical fiction, but it was the fact that I knew that Mills and Boon were looking for new writers. If I'd read that someone was looking for historical romance, I would have gone down that alley, but I didn't.

There is at least one major difference between Penny Jordan's career as a top-selling novelist and those of others: she has never employed a literary agent.

I asked her how, after writing numerous romantic novels, she viewed her good fortune?

I consider that luck was one of the most important factors in my success. I was in the right place and at the right time. There could be a thousand people who could have written that first novel equally as well, or as badly, as I did, but I had the good fortune to send it in at that specific time.

And my luck included a great editor, Jackie Bianchi. She edited my first and subsequent books, but sadly she was killed in a car accident.

It is a curious fact that the titles of Mills and Boon romances do not tend to have the same importance as titles of other genres. (Among Penny's novels are *Bought With His Name*, *Desire's Captive*, *Passionate Protection*, *Stronger Than Yearning* and *Valentines Night*.) Book titles are normally considered very important, as Hailey, Cussler and others stress, but with romantic fiction it is the publisher's reputation and the author's style that matter most.

Sadly, there was no launch party for her first novel; since the publishers produce so many new titles each year, a party for each new novel would be impossible. When *Falcon's Prey* was published, it was just another title among the many on the Mills and Boon shelves. Penny, like all authors, went down to her local bookshop to see it on display. That was very satisfying, but without a party, and without any major coverage in the local papers (and such novels are very rarely reviewed in the national press), her career as an author got off to a very unpretentious start.

Even now, but especially then, it's more the brand-name that counts. People have specific writers that they like or don't like, but it's Mills and Boon that counts, not the writer.

I think it's quite common with Mills and Boon, when they take on a new writer, to have to publish several titles before the writer builds up a following of readers. I really don't know anything of this side of the business, but I think they bring out so many of each one [writer] and they won't know, until they get the returns, how well it's sold or not.

Readers may not be familiar with the term 'returns'. Bookshops generally order books from publishers on a 'sale-or-return' basis, and if after a period some are left unsold, they can be returned to the publisher for credit at the price at which they were bought in. A publisher can thus see a stock of, say, 10,000 copies leave his warehouse, only later to have, if he's unlucky, several thousand copies back. It is as galling for the author as for the publisher, not least because it affects the author's royalty payments.

It takes Penny about a month to complete a novel, though she wilts if it does not fall right first time. She seldom goes back and rewrites, or 'patches', as she calls it. More often she turns her mind to something else, in apparent contradiction of the determination writers need if they are to finish a book.

I don't go over and over it, or rework it. That's just not me, which is why I'm struggling with this long book which I've just done. I'm having to patch and alter it, and it's absolute murder because of the intensity of the concentration.

I do set myself targets. I said it would take me six weeks to complete the corrections and I hope to finish next week. That would be four, and if I don't finish it, all hell breaks loose. If I don't make my own target, I'm unliveable-with.

... I do gabble and rush things, and it's the same when I write. People who know me say they can see a lot of me in the novels, but it's not deliberate.

Often the views that I propound for the heroine may not be specifically mine, but I accept that the characters, such as they are, have a bias towards my own characteristics because it's easier that way. I write more of what I want to write, rather than what I think the public would like to read, but there are things that I would like to write that I haven't written.

Of all my novels, I've enjoyed writing *Loving* the most, but they all must have a happy ending. I wouldn't write anything different, because I like that.

I write what I think is a good story simply because I enjoy writing it, but I have little idea as to why they are so successful.

Someone I know who regularly reads Penny's novels tells me that the men described in her novels are always vulnerable in some way or other; as a result, readers cannot help but feel sorry for them. It may be that other readers identify in some way with her characters and the situations they find themselves in.

Penny writes many more novels than are actually published, for, surprisingly, Mills and Boon sometimes turn her work down. She is the only author I have interviewed to have been regularly published by one firm over a period of years, and yet to have had some of her work rejected (one report quotes her success rate as 80 per cent.) As you will read elsewhere, most authors usually leave their publisher if one of their typescripts is turned down.

Naturally, whenever Mills and Boon reject a novel, they give reasons: 'not enough sparkle', say, or 'the storyline's too heavy for a light romance', all of which can be very helpful to a writer, if somewhat disappointing. Penny told me that she simply 'flings them into a cupboard', since they are of little use to any other publisher, having being written specifically for Mills and Boon. This surprising piece of information started me wondering whether other Mills and Boon authors received the same treatment. If so, there must be hundreds of near publishable typescripts stored away – and suitable, perhaps, for another publisher? It may be that, in an attempt to emulate the world-famous Mills and Boon formula, someone will well publish them one day.

Penny's output is high. Each novel is about 55,000 words, considerably smaller than a conventional novel of around 85,000 words. Clearly, it is difficult to ensure that each new romance has a fresh storyline, and that the plots or characters in any two books do not repeat themselves – what a cynic might call 'the Barbara Cartland syndrome'.

Penny readily confessed that she does not go back and re-read her earlier titles.

There's little point. I can remember the basic plots, but with romance there are only so many – or, if you like, there's only one plot.

I'm probably repeating myself all the time, but it's repeating it with a different story, and with a different set of characters and a different emotional basis. I always emphasise the emotional basis. That's the important thing.

Then I give the heroine a career, as it were. When I worked, they [the novels] often had office settings. Now I'm at home... they tend to have a more country setting. I've one heroine who earns a living doing baskets of dried flowers, and one who repairs tapestries. They have the same story, boy meets girl, and the happy ending, but they are all different.

I don't create the characters as such. They just grow up around the emotion.

I'm influenced by what's going on around me and I'm happy with what I do. For example, I'm not after any literary award. Recognition for me is people going out and buying. I'm not trying to write something of literary merit, I'm trying to write stories. There's a big difference.

Writing perfect English and writing a bestseller are two completely different things. It's like a painting. One can be a beautiful object itself, because of its colour and the way it is constructed. Another can be a painting of a scene that draws you into it. The first stands in its own right for its colour, shape and form [but] – as a literary work – the latter will draw you into it because it will tell a story.

The actual use of the language isn't the primary function; telling a good story is the primary function. If the story holds the reader's attention, it doesn't matter about the language.

To anyone wanting to be a writer, I would say, 'Sit down and do it. Give it a try.' And read a lot.

If you just want to write, you can write what you like. The pleasure is in the writing. But if they want to get it published, if they want to earn a living at it, that's a totally different concept.

I wouldn't recommend anyone to sit down cold-bloodedly and say, 'I want to earn my living writing.' It doesn't work that way.

Penny's view that writing perfect English does not automatically confer bestsellerdom is supported by most of the other authors I interviewed. However, before anyone deduces that any standard will do, they would do well to remember that a typescript has to be easy to read, and that the more editorial work a publisher has to do, the more expensive the book is to produce, and thus the higher its price in the shops. Penny was clearly very fortunate to have her first work published so easily, but luck – although she had already admitted that the timing was important – was not the only factor in her success.

> Then and since, I've had marvellous editors, which is a terrific boon. They do help, but I realise that people might misconstrue this help. People imagine that with Mills and Boon, you are told what to write. That isn't true; you're not. And you are not given a formula and told, 'Here, this is what you can do.'

Penny may not have been given a definitive formula, but Mills and Boon go out of their way to help aspiring writers, perhaps more than any other publisher. The company provides written notes about the so-called formula in an effort to help the author meet current demands of the romance market, and these demands have changed in recent times. One result is that they receive over 4,000 unsolicited typescripts a year, many times more than they publish. They have some 350 authors whom they do publish, whose ages range from the twenties (I believe the youngest ever signed up was eighteen) to the seventies. Interestingly, Mills and Boon report that this is also the age-range of their readership, something that should encourage any reader with even the vaguest of romantic storytelling inclinations.

Once writers are accepted by them, and once their novels have acquired a sound following, they can look forward to seeing at least 100,000 copies printed of each title.

With over 100 titles to her name, worldwide sales of 75 million copies and novels ranked in the top group borrowed from public libraries, Penny has achieved the dreams that so many others harbour. Would-be romantic novelists should take heart from this, and 'have a go'.

Molly Parkin

There cannot be many authors who have had their novels banned from display by W. H. Smith, but that happened to Molly Parkin.

We had real trouble with *Up Tight*. I had asked my old photographer friend, Harri Peccinotti, who worked with me on *Nova*, to photograph a girl for the front cover. What I wanted was a frontal close up of a girl in her knickers, fifties knickers with broderie anglaise and a bit of lace at the bottom. What we ended up with was a girl in knickers all right, but in the see-through seventies style, and with nothing left to the imagination.

No wonder W. H. Smith felt it too risqué to put on the shelves, and no wonder that publishers would not let her choose material for any more jackets.

Sarah Harrison

Carol [Smith, her agent] introduced me to Rosemary de Courcy, an editor at the paperback publishers, Futura. She was looking for books to commission for their Troubadour imprint, which was Futura's new line in 'hot historicals'.

At Carol's office and over lunch we discussed numerous ideas for their Troubadour imprint and these were finally whittled down to three. The only trouble was that they were all for historical novels, and history is not something I'm good at. Rosie was looking for someone to write about the First World War, but from a woman's point of view. That's the one I decided to work on and when I sent in my thirty-page synopsis, I was still doubtful whether it would be good enough. They accepted it and agreed on their standard advance: two thousand pounds.

That was probably very good, but to me it was riches, it was the most money I'd seen. I got one thousand pounds on signature and one thousand on delivery.

Rosemary de Courcy was actually looking for an author to follow the popular 'bodice-ripping' successes of 'hot' historical sagas. She and Futura's managing director, Anthony Cheetham, saw this new genre of fiction not only as a potential money-spinner but, if they could find a bestseller in this new field, as something that would establish Futura as a market leader. Sarah seemed just the right author for them.

It was at about this time that Sarah had another real break, when she entered a literary competition. This time it was for a children's book, and was sponsored by *The Sunday Times*. The winning entry would be illustrated by Nicola Bayley, and would be published. Despite the realisation that there were likely to be some 60,000 entrants, Sarah thought she would have a go.

I never really stood a chance, you know, with all those entries, but I spent the best part of half a day on it, and of course I didn't win. It's very hard to get a children's book right. Then it sat on my agent's desk for many weeks afterwards while she wondered what to do with it. Then quite by chance an impecunious illustrator from the Hornsey College of Art came to her office asking if there was anything he could demonstrate his talents on. She said, 'Well, I've got this. Why not take this away?' Two days later he returned with the most wonderful pictures. They were absolutely beautiful and then we sold *In Granny's Garden* to Jonathan Cape within a week. The illustrator was Mike Wilks. He's a very successful man now. He did *The Ultimate Alphabet Book*, which was in the bestseller list for weeks. Now he lives in the south of France and you almost can't get to talk to him now without an appointment.

You know, the people who make money want to write serious well-reviewed books, and people who write serious well-reviewed books want to make money. I would just like to write a life-enhancing novel, but I do not know what the hell it would be. Usually when people say that, it means that they feel that they're not fulfilling their potential, or they are not doing what they could. Whereas I have a nasty suspicion that I have.

My advice to any aspiring author is, I think, not to stop writing. I think people put their all into one short thing and send it off and wait for the result, instead of immediately writing something else. I know it sounds terribly banal, but if you keep the muscle working, it's better.

Dora Saint ('Miss Read')

*Best known, under her pen-name 'Miss
Read', for Village School, Battles at Thrush
Green, No Holly for Miss Quinn, Village
Affairs, Gossip from Thrush Green, At
Home in Thrush Green, and 59 more.*

DORA SAINT IS a truly English author, unassuming
and unpretentious, avoiding, like Penny Jordan,
the limelight of hype and publishers' publicity.
She prefers instead to live in the heart of England's
countryside where she can lead a rural life in
harmony with nature. Nevertheless, her books are
widely read and loved; proof, perhaps, that word-of-
mouth recommendation does work. Her popularity
is reflected by her regular ranking as one of the
authors whose books are most borrowed from
British libraries. In recent years, she has earned
the maximum possible under the Public Lending
Right agreement.

For her, as for several other authors, writing is a
second career, but unlike, say, those of Dick Francis
or Jeffrey Archer, her first career was not one that

attracted either headlines or public attention. She was, as she told me, simply 'an uncomplicated teacher'. Her success is thus the more significant, and must surely encourage other writers.

Dora Saint's home, in a country house near the village of Great Shefford in the Berkshire Down, in well manicured and colourful gardens, is a haven for the local bird population for nuts and titbits are always available. Her love for the countryside and her passion for rural traditions is obvious to any visitor.

Dora's empathy with the countryside originates from her early childhood. Brought up in South London, her first experience of school was at a typical London County Council establishment; fifty to a class, a concrete playground and surrounded by noise. This was not to last, for in 1921, when she was seven years old, the family moved to Chelsfield. The village lies close to the Kent border in what was a fruit growing area. It was a time when children could walk to school in relative safety, and for Dora this meant a mile or so along country lanes. What made the greatest impact were the sights and sounds of nature, of animals and birds and the smells of crops and wild flowers. She loved it all.

This fascination explains why, many years later, she enjoys writing about country life; it is a subject she knows well. Her books are renowned for portraying rural and, in particular, village life in England as we should all like to remember it, especially in the south, where it is rapidly disappearing beneath the mass of urban developments.

Dora Saint has a unique ability to let her readers see and share her world. She could also very easily be the 'Miss Read' of her novels. Matronly in appearance, she inspires confidence and oozes good sense. Above all else, she is a practical and level-headed person, qualities you would expect of a headmistress.

So why did she start to write? Was it something that she, like so many others, had always dreamt of doing, or was it a side-effect of teaching?

> When I was at school, I had great difficulty in anything connected with mathematics and so on, but on the expression side, I found it fairly simple. I always thought, like thousands of other people, one day I'll do a bit of writing. Certainly, I wanted to be a reporter on a paper when I was in my teens. That would have been bliss.

And I said so to my father. He was horrified, and he said (and I'll always remember his expression), he said, 'That's much too rackety a life for a girl.' So I went into teaching instead.

I had quite a few years as a teacher, but later when I had time, after I was married, I used to think about the idiotic remarks you made when you were teaching. I recall, when teaching infants and getting up a little play, that I said, 'I'm looking for two trustworthy frogs.' I thought, I must be mad; I mean, what would they think? It was that sort of thing that sounded amusing, so by that time I had definitely decided to try my hand at a light essay.

One of the most prestigious magazines at the time was *Punch*. It also had an element of humour, so I thought I would try *Punch* first. It was hard work, but I used to send them something about once a fortnight and, as regularly, they came back, sometimes with a comment or two which helped.

I wasn't upset that my efforts were not accepted to begin with. I went on the principle that you must expect to be rejected. I thought that this was a sensible way to face it. And it's the advice I give to any beginners, so that if you are accepted, the joy is doubled.

And after trying for about eighteen months, they took a little article called 'Last Week's Film'. This was followed by several other small articles, but I remember 'Plasticine for Forty' was the beginning of a series of articles about the humorous aspects of teaching.

They were virtually all monologues. Me talking to a class of forty children about their plasticine, saying idiotic things like, 'Hold up worms'; 'Hold up baskets'. And comments like 'It's time you put that down, you've done sixteen crumpets already'; 'Well, turn it over and make the holes on the other side.' The sort of thing that the late Joyce Grenfell would say.

H. F. Ellis, who was the literary and deputy editor of *Punch* from 1949 to 1953, recalled in *The Sunday Telegraph* in 1978:

She was one of my favourite contributors because she had no arrogance at all and didn't feel her work was sacrosanct – in fact, I think she was very aware that at about eight hundred words her pieces were extremely useful editorially, and never minded revising them. In a way, she was, and is, like Jane Austen, in that she writes about what she knows and never goes beyond it.

SAGAS AND ROMANCE

I next asked Dora when it was that her career as a writer had really taken off. Was it in the fifties?

> No, it was the late forties. About 1947. I tried to widen my scope a bit. When the articles came back from *Punch*, I used to try sending them elsewhere, naturally. Sometimes I was lucky, but often not because writing for *Punch* was very particular. I did occasionally get things into *The Lady* and *Country Life*, then *The Times Educational Supplement* wrote asking if I would do some reviewing for them, which I did.
>
> After a while, I said to the editor [of the *TES*], 'It's about time you had a light essay in your paper. I'm doing articles about town and country schools for *Punch* at the moment.'
>
> 'Send me some, then, and let me have a look at them'; which I did, and he told me that he would have had this, and that... I started regularly for the *Times Ed*. and I must say they never sent anything back. They were wonderful.

Though it did not fulfil her teenage dream of becoming a reporter, to many would-be writers, such a job would be very welcome. Her work was seldom credited to her by name, and only occasionally by her initials, D.J.S.; an aspect that would disappoint most writers at the start of their career.

But she was certainly blazing a trail, for it was then unheard-of for the *'Times Ed.'* to carry essays. Persuading the paper to start publishing these was, in retrospect, the turning-point in her writing career, not least because it led to her next big break. Felicity Kinross of the BBC Schools Department asked her to write a script or two for their radio programmes. As it turned out, this was not a one-off request, and she wrote for the BBC on a regular basis for several years. It was a piece she published in the *Observer*, however, 'Thirty-One and a Donkey', that caught the eye of Bob [the late Sir Robert] Lusty, then working at Michael Joseph. In November 1953 Lusty asked her to call on him at his office. It proved to be yet another turning-point, as she recalled in the book published to celebrate Michael Joseph's fiftieth anniversary, *At The Sign Of The Mermaid* (1986):

> ... and Robert Lusty asked which papers I had appeared in.
>
> '*Punch, The Countryman, The Times Educational Supplement, The Lady.*'
>
> 'Quite reputable papers,' he said meditatively.

'Really quite reputable.'

'Short essays, of course. Not much more than eight-hundred-and-fifty words. How long should a book be?'

'Oh! About seventy thousand,' he said casually.

I fell back, stunned, upon the mini-sofa. When I had struggled up again, I said I could not possibly write so much.

'Why ever not?' he asked, astonished. 'You won't find the length difficult once you begin.'

He continued to try and reassure me until we parted.

In numbed despair I sought normality in Dryad's craft shop next door, among the wooden beads and raffia.

And a week later I started on *Village School*...

Dora recalls that, when they met, Lusty said to her, 'We're not commissioning you to do this job, but if you would like to write a book, we shall look at it with interest.' After he had accepted the book, he pointed out that she was not yet a 'known author', so perhaps she ought to use a pen-name. He suggested 'Miss Read' as it was written in the first person, which, for a book about school life, sounded most apt. 'Make it more of an autobiography,' he had added, though he could not have guessed just how her enchanting and evocative stories of rural life would capture the imagination of millions. Cynics might say that this was a piece of publisher's luck, others that it was a stroke of publisher's genius. Either way, it is a prime example of a publisher recognising that intangible quality which sets one author apart from others.

Lusty was never to commission Dora Saint, neither then, nor for any of the titles that followed. Granted that commissioning fiction was not the convention then, and especially fiction by an unknown author, it is still very surprising that once she was successful, her publishers did not feel it necessary to bind her to them with contracts. However, like the majority of publishers' contracts then, there was a clause in hers that gave Michael Joseph the first option on her next title. So once a contract had been issued for a book she had delivered, she did have a publisher to turn to, which pleased her. Michael Joseph have published every title since the first.

I asked Dora if she thought of sending her first book to any other publisher.

No, I didn't. But when I sent the first five or six chapters to Bob, he was rather lacklustre about it. He said it hadn't got the sparkle of the essays. Naturally it hadn't, which I quite appreciated.

For one thing, I was feeling my way and desperately worried about the length of the book. Was I using up too much material in those five chapters? Was I not putting enough in? I simply did not know. I was used to a journalistic approach, very astringent. I was really at sea with the length.

That's why I divided the book into three terms, the school year, and each term into eight chapters. That way, I got some idea of how much I was putting into each chapter. That was my bannister all through that first book.

This approach to 'pacing' a novel is sound advice for anyone planning to write a book. Her novels are, on average, about 65–70,000 words long, and make about 220 pages in paperback form. Her methodical structuring of her books has not only been a major help to Dora in maintaining pace, but it also makes for much easier storytelling.

To achieve this, Dora turned to something familiar – the school exercise book. Writing her novels longhand, she planned to end a chapter by the time she reached the staples in the middle and finish the next chapter by the last page. Thus twelve books would make a full-length novel.

Most of her 'original manuscripts' have since been bound into volumes and they are a testimony to her precise style of writing for there are hardly any corrections or amendments to be found!

Village School was finished in October 1954 and published the following year; it was the first of more than fifty titles published over the next 51 years. Since then, none of them has been out of print for long. 'Miss Read's' success is all the more remarkable because, unlike other authors setting out on their second career, she did not have an agent to help her, nor did she have the benefit of a 'literary' spouse.

Village School was favourably reviewed in several papers. Her old employer at the *The Times Educational Supplement* telephoned her, congratulating her and pulling her leg at the same time. She had achieved a hat-trick, he told her: her first book had appeared in concurrent issues of *The Times*, *The Times Literary Supplement* and *The Times Higher Educational Supplement*. It was an intoxicating moment, though 'Miss Read' was then, and remains, 'anaesthetised and remote from reviews'.

About reviews generally, and this may sound conceited but it is not, and I think you'll find a lot of writers are like this. By the time you have done the book, you are not at all interested in it. So, if they praise the book, you're very pleased, you're grateful; and if they slam it, you don't really care much because you are not really interested in it any more. It's the book that you are currently working on that matters.

Many authors I've met are convinced that to become successful, writers must discipline themselves to work at a regular time each day; indeed, this is necessary just to complete a novel, they believe. 'Do you set yourself a routine for writing?' I asked.

No. But determination is the main thing. To my mind you've simply got to plug on, and keep on, and on and on. If you are going to write, and you want to be accepted and marketed, you've not got to take any notice of rejections.

As a housewife, and as a mum in the earlier days, I found I couldn't possibly keep to office hours. In any case, part of the time I was teaching. Only here and there. But if they wanted a supply teacher in any nearby rural school, I would push off for a week while someone was away ill. So, for a time, it was a very fragmented life I was leading.

On a good day, I write for about three hours in the mornings, but the hours are very varied.

I used to tell Bob Lusty, or Michael Joseph, that I would finish the book by March, or April, and give myself a certain leeway. That would allow me to take holidays, and not to worry too much if my daughter was ill and I had to take time off to look after her. I could never work a nine-to-five routine.

These comments are very significant, coming from the author of more than fifty books. They are, too, at variance with the views of the majority of successful writers.

Fans of 'Miss Read' will know all about the two villages she created, Thrush Green and Fairacre. Most of her novels recount the daily happenings of family life in these villages in the days before such places succumbed to modern 'amenities'. Each book takes the story of their lives a step further. These are fictional villages and characters, but where did she get all her ideas and material?

About ninety-five per cent of the material comes from my memories. If I come across something technical that I don't understand, I seek help. For instance, in one book, I wanted a public enquiry. That was all Greek to me, so I started to telephone people I thought might help. The town clerk provided the answers. I must say that people are marvellous about telling you the proceedings. And the same thing happened when I wanted to find out recently how, at a police station, an identity parade would be held.

I have never had any difficulty in getting help, but generally I write about what I know.

I do wonder, however, whether this sort of help is always so freely available to the aspiring author, although clearly that must depend on the subject chosen.

Something which has fascinated me throughout all these interviews, and which I am sure has crossed the minds of many readers, is why some authors who have written regularly over a period of many years remain popular, while others do not. 'Miss Read' is one of those few authors who, while following the same theme throughout her books, has engendered, and kept, a loyal readership. I wondered why?

HOW TO BE A BESTSELLING NOVELIST

First of all, there is this great basic longing for the country in everybody. Certainly the people who read my books have it.

My novels have a collection of characters that's not too big, and anybody with any 'savvy' knows that you don't want a great big cast when you are writing something to hold your reader's interest. All my characters have ongoing lives and it's the serial aspect in my books, just as it is with *The Archers* on the radio, that holds the reader's attention. They want to know what happens next.

I've got the human element, and the countryside background, and from my point of view you're then halfway there.

But I'm not good at plots. I start with place first of all, then I consider the characters. There are collections of characters in both villages, and I find that I can make perhaps one person the theme of that book. In one of my recent books, it was the two schoolteachers at Thrush Green and their adventures that became the main story; how they were going to retire and how they couldn't find a house. Then I brought in other people to keep them in the reader's eye, as well as covering the main story.

> Above all, I consider the reader. I'm conscious
> of keeping the reader's attention very clearly.

'Miss Read' obviously writes on the subject she knows and loves best. The dilemma facing many aspiring writers is whether to tackle a subject they know nothing about, because they imagine that it might make a good story; or to write about their own experiences, which they feel may interest people, but which seldom do.

I once read in *The Writer's Handbook* that Ruth Rendell had posed the question: '. . . I wonder where I would be now if I had aimed to please a public rather than suited my own taste?' But further on, Samm Sinclair Baker advised in an article 'How To Sell': 'Write what interests most others, not just what pleases you.' This conflict of views will doubtless remain unresolved.

The novels of 'Miss Read' will surely go on selling for many years to come, but which title, I wondered, had given her the most satisfaction?

> Oh, without doubt, *Village School*. It has also been
> the most successful, possibly because it was the
> first one and people, if they want to start reading

me, go naturally to *Village School*.

I'm told, some years ago, my books have passed the two million mark, and a number have been translated into German, Japanese and Russian. Surprisingly, they sell well in America. I get a lot of letters from there. I don't know why, possibly because they like to find their roots, and that sort of thing.

I receive several hundred letters a year, about a dozen a week or so, and I answer all of them by hand. I very rarely get a critical one, but once I received a letter to tell me that one of my characters had committed bigamy on page 247! I checked, and he certainly had, so I replied that I would be putting this right before the next printing. That character now dies in an air crash.

Writing a book is very hard work; it takes me at least eight to ten months to finish one and it nearly kills me! I feel very guilty if I haven't written...

Dora Saint's novels evoke nostalgic emotions in all those readers who have spent some or all of their lives in the countryside, and in readers who long for the country and an escape from the hectic pace of modern life. Here, then, is a lesson that aspiring writers might take note of – that to win a mass readership, books must appeal to the masses.

So what advice would she offer someone aiming to become an author?

Well, I should be completely practical about it, and tell them to write a synopsis about what they've got in mind. Send it with a covering letter to the first publisher they think would like to have their book. If they express an interest, then go ahead and do it.

I would say, keep the thing as simple as possible, not only in language but in format. Keep the reader in mind.

Be practical too. Don't send a horror story to a publisher of agricultural books. Send it to the right publisher.

...ays write from the heart.

· Strong central character
· Sub-plot?

THINGS TO CONSIDER
· Finding an agent
· Overcoming writer's block
... writer should always
... a notebook & pen.

Part 3

Adventure writers

Jeffrey Archer

While he was in dire financial straits, several people prompted him to write a book. One of those was David Niven, the son of the late, and much-loved, film actor. Jeffrey records his appreciation for the younger Niven's help at the beginning of *Not A Penny More, Not A Penny Less*. He added:

> I wanted to make a film originally and I didn't think I could write. So I wrote fifty pages for him [Niven]. It may have been twenty-five, but it was a very small number. I sent it to him, he read it and said, 'It will make a fantastic book, Jeffrey, but you must not sell it to a film company, because if you do, they will pay you five-hundred or a thousand pounds, for the idea. They will do it themselves and no one will ever believe you had anything to do with it at all.'
> I said, 'I'm not capable of writing a book.'
> 'Nevertheless,' he replied, 'go and do it.'

He made a simple decision to write a novel, one that just had to be a bestseller. He believed that producing a bestseller was nothing to do with writing, it was all to do with telling stories – something he was able to do.

What sets Jeffrey Archer apart from all the other authors I interviewed is that he sat down to write a novel that would make him a fortune. He was not interested in just being published, in seeing his name on the spine of a book.

I always say to people who write to me, you must get away from your husband, or wife. Go away, or get rid of them. You can't write just after breakfast and just before lunch. Maybe at the weekend. You have got to write your first draft flat out for six weeks, or four weeks, or whatever it takes you, and any interference is only going to stop the flow and get it wrong.

Otherwise, you will produce a piece of work even you will admit is not good enough. The one thing you must do, is to write the best you can do, and if you fail, well at least you can say you gave it your best shot. If you say you could have made it much better, that's no good to anyone.

I also think it should be a second career, not the first. Thirty-three or thirty-four would be an ideal age to start.

Tom Clancy

*The Hunt For Red October, Red Storm
Rising, Patriot Games, The Cardinal of
the Kremlin, Clear and Present Danger,
The Sum of All Fears, Without Remorse,
Debt of Honour, Executive Orders, Marine,
The Teeth of the Tiger and others.*

In 1984, Tom Clancy was a full-time insurance
salesman. He had his own business, which
specialised in selling policies on cars and boats; at
that time, the idea of writing a book remained a
schoolboy dream. Nowadays all that is behind him,
for he is a full-time writer with many bestsellers to
his credit.

He has earned himself a unique reputation for
writing tales all too authentic and chilling – which
display a detailed knowledge not only of current
military intelligence, but also of little-known
contemporary strategy. 'All too authentic', experts
felt, because his detailed descriptions of submarines,
especially Russia's then state-of-the-art nuclear
Typhoon Class, and of America's stealth aircraft were
far too accurate for their peace of mind.

When *The Hunt For Red October* was published in 1984, John Lechman, then US Navy Secretary, is believed to have thundered to colleagues, having read the book, 'Who the hell cleared this?' Other officials commented, too. US Secretary of Defense Caspar W. Weinberger, whose job it was to know about such matters, occasionally reviewed books. Of Tom's novel he wrote, in the *International Herald Tribune*:

> There are lots of spy novels, and novels involving military technology, but I don't call to mind many, if any, that compare to Clancy's *Hunt For Red October*; based on accuracy, ability to communicate, narrative skills and plot. It's hard to stop reading this book.

And when *Red Storm Rising* came out in 1986 the technical details were so realistic that the Pentagon suspected that the author had seen classified material.

Tom Clancy stresses, however, that all the so-called secrets he exposed are available through sources officially accessible to the public. Clancy's are an exposé of future warfare using today's hardware. His readers could be forgiven for believing that Tom has years of military service behind him. That is not the case, however, for he was excused service, having been born with severe myopia.

Neither in high school, nor at Loyola College in Baltimore, did he give any indication of the huge successes to come.

> I didn't set any records at college. It's true I did get a degree in English, but that's due to the encouragement of the teachers. I don't think there's an English teacher in the world that doesn't encourage you to write. All mine did. And there were a lot of good teachers, some Jesuits and some civilians...
>
> I wasn't into sports, because I wasn't terribly well co-ordinated. I was also a puny little kid. I didn't really finish growing up until college. And I was just a scrawny guy in high school.
>
> Despite the encouragement, I didn't get involved in *Blue and Gold*, the school literary magazine, but I did have some stories published in it.

Authors whose early literary efforts appear in school magazines sometimes turn to writing letters to local newspapers. Did he, I wondered, do the same?

No I didn't, and I didn't want to become a reporter. My dad did not like reporters very much. Sports reporters especially. It greatly annoyed him that he had to pay for his football tickets, and they got in for free. And he knew the game better than they did.

So I never held the journalistic profession in high esteem until I actually got to meet some of the people in the business. They turned out to be some pretty good folks. My first exposure to reporters was after all this success, and for the most part, the people I have met have been pretty damn good...

When I went to England for the first time, I was disappointed by the newspapers over there because they are so small. I mean, they are puny little things compared to what we have here, but I was impressed by the prose. You guys evidently have better English teachers. The depth of coverage was kind of disappointing, although your James Adams, on *The Sunday Times*, is probably the best defence reporter in the whole world.

If journalism was out, what had made him take up a career in insurance?

I graduated from college in 1969, and my wife and I were engaged to be married on second August of '69. I needed a job in a hurry, and it was simply the first decent job offer I received. But in 1980 I took over the business and by the time I had, it paid off the loans, and by 1985, I didn't need it any more.

But I wasn't the best insurance agent in the world; I mean, I made a living and met my payroll. Fundamentally, it took me thirty-five years to find my niche is writing. Writing is the first really disciplined activity that I've been able to do.

No doubt the success of *The Hunt For Red October* helped confirm this view. Once again, however, here is evidence that it is very important for an aspiring author to have a full-time job until he or she has become established as a writer.

Tom Clancy was in his early thirties in 1985, and he had what most of us would call a comfortable life ahead of him. He had a steady job, a loving wife and two children, two cars, a mortgage, of course, and all the other commitments and constraints that go with family life. His job had its ups and downs, but by and large it treated him well. So what was it that made him seek the challenge of writing a novel?

Quite simply, he told me, it came about because, during one of his rare moments of idleness, he began to ponder on what he had achieved in his life. This is something that everyone does from time to time, but in his case he realised that he was caught in a middle-class trap of his own making, and that there was no easy way out of it. He would have to remain where he was in order to earn enough to maintain the payments and meet all his other commitments.

In 1986, Father Sellinger of Loyola College, noting Tom's success, invited him to address that year's graduates. This was the moment at which Tom focused his mind in an effort to account for his sudden change in life. He told them:

> There is a defence against the trap into which you are all about to embark, and the defence is within yourselves... Nothing is as real as a dream. The world can change around you, but your dream will not. Your life may change, but your dream doesn't have to. Responsibilities need not erase it. Duties need not obscure it. Your spouse and children need not get in its way, because the dream is within you. No-one can take your dream away.

This may explain his motive for extricating himself from the self-generated rut, but it was his life-long love of military hardware that provided the impetus for his new career as a storyteller. He had the necessary attributes of a thriller-writer: a vivid imagination, a proven ability in English, and a new slant on a storyline. Some years earlier – on 8 November 1975, as he recalled – he had read a most unusual news item. Members of the crew of the Soviet frigate *Storozhevoy* had decided to defect to Sweden, though most of them were killed in the mutiny. Because the story was so out of the ordinary, it stuck in Tom's memory. In time, his imagination converted the frigate into a submarine, and the plot for *The Hunt for Red October* began to take shape.

As Tom's interest in the United States Navy grew, he bought more and more books on that and allied subjects. His growing appetite for anything about naval history, defence trends, and maritime affairs led him to join the United States Naval Institute, whose headquarters, conveniently, are based in nearby Annapolis. The Institute publishes a wide range of authoritative titles under the Naval Institute Press imprint, and since members of the Institute are allowed to buy those books at discounted prices, he saw a distinct advantage in becoming a member.

In April 1980 he went to the Institute's annual meeting. What he heard and saw there was to have a profound effect on him.

> I saw essentially a kind of great big exercise in informational incest, where people in the Navy were telling each other how important the Navy is. Hell, they already know that. The idea is that they should tell the taxpayers how important the Navy is, then they'll support the people in uniform.

So incensed was he by the occasion that he wrote an 800-word article for the Institute's journal, *Proceedings*, in which he castigated the admirals and the speakers alike, and called much of the meeting 'a singular waste of time'. Considering that he also reproached the Institute for not promoting the Navy's importance, it is perhaps surprising and greatly to their credit that they supported him so strongly in an accompanying column. Naturally, one effect of the article, and of the fuss it caused, was to put Tom Clancy's name firmly on the map.

This was one of two articles that he had published in *Proceedings*. The other, a three-page piece on the MX missile, appeared in July 1982. Apart from these, he had had nothing published since college, and was anything but the archetypal author.

I didn't have sufficient intelligence to know that it was a matter of confidence. There's an old Japanese proverb, 'A blind man fears no snakes.' I just went ahead, not knowing what the problems were.

I thought that was as far as that letter and article would get, but the following year, I met a naval officer, Ralph Chatham, who offered some criticism. So I invited him down to my office. This was on the Monday, after Argentina had just gobbled up the Falkland Islands. [Friday 2 April 1982.]

Ralph's a sub driver by profession, and we got talking. He told me some sea stories, about life at sea, and what it was like to drive a submarine for a living.

Well, the idea for *Red October* had been rattling around in my head for some years, and on the basis of the stories he told me, I figured I could write the book. I knew I could look up the technical stuff easily enough; the hard part was getting into the heads of the guys who drive a submarine for a living.

Tom Clancy's knowledge of submarines, fighter aircraft, and other weaponry is authoritative. He understands missiles, for example, in the same way, that dedicated motor-racing fans know their cars, or that computer buffs know their chips. Like so many such aficionados, his interest started in his youth.

I've been a technology freak all my life, back to when I was in first grade. Gadgets fascinate me.

Historically, military technology tends to give a leading edge. If you look at the history of aviation, all the important events in aviation have come from the military side and spread over into the civilian side.

Medicine's the same way. One of the hot items in the United States is trauma treatment; treating people who are shot, or crunched up in automobile accidents. If you are going to get mashed up in an automobile accident, this is the best place in the world, here in Maryland, because they will fly you to the shock trauma centre in Baltimore. A lot of the technicians there came out of the Vietnam War.

Committed to writing a novel, Tom began his research, reading a variety of unclassified books which, though they were not to be found on booksellers' shelves, were nevertheless available to the public. He also bought a war game, *Harpoon*. This had been devised by Larry Bond, a naval analyst, and the accompanying rule book explained a strategy for war between American and Soviet fleets of nuclear-powered submarines and other vessels. This strategy, which was used by the Navy's cadets in training, was most helpful to Tom as an important source of reference data, but he had little idea at that time as to what it was like to live and work in nuclear submarines, or, for that matter, how nuclear power worked. Not far from where he lives, however, there is a nuclear power station. Through some of his insurance company's policy-holders, several of whom were ex-submariners working there, he was able to acquire the vital background details that make his novels so convincingly accurate.

Two years after that fateful annual meeting at the United States Naval Institute, he began to write *The Hunt For Red October*. Two drafts later, he sent it off to the only publisher with whom he had had any contact, the Naval Institute Press. Their forte, however, was (and is) largely academic non-fiction with an emphasis on all matters naval, and fiction was not a feature of their lists. True, he had been encouraged to finish his novel by one of their technical experts, but that was no guarantee of publication.

What he was not aware of, though, was that they had made a major decision to start publishing 'wet' fiction, an unusual move for a publishing house so steeped in traditional non-fiction books. The board had set standards, of course, and it had been agreed that any novel taken on must not only be well written, but should make a contribution to naval literature and advance the understanding of sea power. Tom's novel met these criteria. Delighted to have his work accepted for publication, he readily took the Naval Institute Press's editorial advice, making a number of changes at their suggestion.

At the time, I didn't think I had sent it to the wrong publisher, because I never anticipated the degree of sales that we were going to have.

They did, but I didn't. The only thing that made me think about going to another publisher was when they told me that the Board of Control [equivalent to a board of directors] might vote not to accept the book. And after going through six months of submission and rewrite... they finally accepted the book, and offered me an advance of three thousand dollars. I talked them up to five thousand dollars, but I make a little bit more than that now!

Tom Clancy was really very lucky indeed for, by convention at least, he was doing it all wrong. Not being a well-known – or even a proven – author, he was, on the evidence available, submitting it to the wrong type of publisher. Nor did he have a literary agent, something which, while not essential, does tend to be an asset. He just had a conviction – like so many writers – that he would one day succeed in getting his work published.

The initial printing was 16,000 hardback copies, which is very high compared with the UK's average of about 2,000 for a first novel. Demand rose swiftly, and two reprints each of 5,000 copies were put in hand shortly after the initial printing. Tom thinks that by the end of 1984 his publishers had printed about 30,000 copies.

But can this runaway success be entirely put down to luck? All publishers send out review copies, and NIP were no exception. But they were comparative strangers to publishing fiction, and because *The Hunt For Red October* was the first novel on their list, they gave the book more publicity and promotion than their traditional non-fiction titles usually received. Copies were sent to senior naval and diplomatic personnel, as well as recognised reviewers. Amongst these was Reid Beddow, an editor for the *Washington Post's Book World*, who wrote a very favourable review. Promotional copies of new author's works tend to get passed around faster than more mundane books, if only to show that the donor has 'found' a good new read, and in this case, because the book exposed much of current naval intelligence and strategy, it was passed around the nation's military leaders with alacrity. Tom recalled:

> Jeremiah O'Leary, an editor with the *Washington Times*, received a copy, read it, and liked what he read. He went out and bought a copy for his friend Frank Cortez, the American Ambassador

to Argentina. He in turn gave the book to another friend, Nancy Clark Reynolds, who was flying out there, to drop off at the embassy. This was in November 1984 and on the flight she read it, and liked it too.

When she returned to the States, it was the Christmas season, so she bought a whole case of books to give out as Christmas presents. One went to the President, because she was an old friend of the Reagan family.

The President took two or three days to read the book. It was quiet that Christmas. When he told *Time* magazine that he liked it, boom! It just went. It jumped on the bestseller list in March of '85 and stayed there for twenty-nine weeks as a hardcover. Then the hardcover was knocked off by the paperback. That was pure luck.

A few good reviews undoubtedly help, but a personal recommendation from the nation's leader is the ultimate accolade. Reagan's admiring comments worked wonders, not so much because he was the President, but because he was a man who enjoyed the full-time attention of the media, so that many of the millions of supporters who had elected him took notice.

Word-of-mouth recommendation, especially amongst political and military opinion-formers, helped Clancy win the battle for supremacy in sales.

> I'm convinced that word of mouth is the only factor that sells anything. I guess TV advertising sells soap and Kleenex and that sort of thing, but in the book field, you don't advertise on TV.
>
> The only advertising for books is someone buying a book and reading it, saying, 'Hey, this is pretty good', and telling the guy on the next desk. The plain truth is that I don't think that anybody anywhere knows how to sell a thing...
>
> The only book review that counts is the one you get from the public, and the obligation you have as an author is that when someone spends twenty dollars, or whatever, on buying your book, then he's getting his money's worth. I'm in the entertainment business.
>
> What is writing, but entertainment?

Tom has been described as a 'war gamer', a devotee of hypothetical or historical warfare played out on computers or on boards, usually as a hobby, although the military use war games in training. It was his friendship with Larry Bond, who devised the war game, *Harpoon*, that helped him towards starting his next book, *Red Storm Rising*. Not only did Larry Bond became a good friend, he become the godfather of Clancy's son, Tommy; their common interest, apart from Tommy, lay with war games.

Larry's a good guy and takes his role as godfather very seriously. He was over for Tommy's first birthday party in '83, and in a quiet moment he started talking about a little project he had going called *Convoy 84* which was going to be an extended war game. Testing to see what it was like to get convoys across the North Atlantic in the face of modern weapons, air-to-surface missiles, nuclear submarines, and all that.

We started kicking ideas back and forth, and I said, 'Hell, I've just finished one book. This sounds like fun. Why don't you and me write a book, on this subject, doing a damned war game?' He agreed, and we shook hands on the deal and that was it.

Essentially, it's used as a database, and the game is played at military colleges all over the world. It comes complete with a rule book and technical digest...

That handshake was to prove to be another money-spinner, but although they agreed to share the earnings, only Tom's name appears on copies of *Red Storm Rising*.

Brimming with enthusiasm, Tom is someone who believes in doing rather than talking about doing. With one book just published, he did not wait to be commissioned before starting his second. Meanwhile, elsewhere in the close-knit community of publishing, literary agents were as usual on the prowl for rising stars.

I remember that I met Rob Gottlieb, who eventually became my agent, on Memorial Day [30] May 1984. I was at the American Booksellers' Convention at the time. He had got hold of some galley proofs [of *The Hunt For Red October*], and liked them so much that he went out of his way to find me. In fact he chased me, just like a gigolo chases an heiress, for the next six months or so. I finally signed up with him in January 1985.

The deal I had with Rob was that he could represent us (I was working with Larry Bond) to everybody except the [Naval] Institute [Press]. We would represent ourselves to them. Further, if the Institute came within twenty per cent of the offer we got from the trade, then we could give the book [*Red Storm Rising*] to the Institute.

So we sent off the same package of material, both to the Institute and to Rob, who then sent it off to G. P. Putnam's Sons. And Putnam came back with an original offer of three-hundred-and-twenty-five-thousand dollars.

Any aspiring author should note that these events took place about three months after *The Hunt For Red October* had hit the bookshops. It is worth remembering, too, that his first novel, which had attracted an advance of just $5,000, had not, at the time Putnam made their offer, yet appeared on the bestseller lists! Either Rob Gottlieb was a very effective agent, or Putnam's management were more than alert to the potential of *Red Storm Rising*. Nevertheless, Tom went back to his publisher at the Naval Institute Press:

'Look,' I said, standing in the doorway, 'this is the offer we have received.'

'They offered you three-hundred-and-twenty-five-thousand dollars for that?' was my publisher's response. I was a little offended by that, by his reaction, in fact. I then said, 'Do you want to make an offer?' He just said 'No.'

'You're sure?' I asked. 'Why don't you come within twenty per cent, and you can have the book?'

They declined, and so another publisher won the day and the golden prize. On the face of it, his original publishers seem to have thrown away a first class opportunity to make money, but there is another side to the tale. The Naval Institute Press is governed by its non-profit tax status, and is precluded from making any monetary offer, regardless of size, in competition with a commercial, and therefore tax-paying, publisher. In offering to let his second book go to the Naval Institute Press at twenty per cent less than the best offer, Tom seemed generous though he would, of course, not be paying fees to his agent.

And, curiously, the contract for his first novel did not have a 'first option' clause, which obliges a writer to offer his next book to his publishers before offering it elsewhere.

Tom's experience with his second novel is a powerful argument for employing an agent. Some authors seem to endorse their involvement, whilst others shun them like the plague. On balance, much depends on whether a writer has the confidence, the knowledge, and the business acumen to deal with publishers, and even then it is most unlikely that a first-time author would have the sort of reputation in publishing that the best agents command.

I met Tom Clancy at his home in Maryland. He writes not in some small corner but in what most readers would describe as a library. His must have held several thousand titles. Three walls are covered with bookshelves from floor to ceiling, so that he has to use a ladder to reach the upper shelves. He clearly likes books – books on all subjects – though there is, of course, a predominance of military books. His fascination with military history began when he was very young, but his interest in weapons and military memorabilia is also clear: he proudly showed me several handguns he had lying around the room, as well as military caps and other mementoes. Photographs of himself aboard fighting ships adorned the wall, as did several of President Reagan, each bearing a personal inscription.

One of Clancy's laws of writing is that you always have to kill somebody in the first chapter. The first chapter, or the first sentence, has to grab the reader.

Red Storm starts off, 'They moved swiftly, silently, with purpose, under a crystalline, star-filled night in western Siberia.' And *Patriot Games* starts, 'Ryan was nearly killed twice in half an hour.' What you want to do is to get the reader to think, 'hey, what's going on here?'

You can always come up with a reason not to work today. I mean, no matter what you do, whether you drive a truck, or you're an accountant, or a cop, you can always come up with a perfectly good reason why you should stay at home and do something else. It's the same thing for a writer. I suppose the principal requirement for a writer is determination.

I start when the kids get kicked out of the house by eight o'clock on their way to school. I start off by editing what I did the previous day. This sort of gets your brain synchronised with what you are supposed to be doing. I work through to lunch. I sometimes work a little after lunch, but generally, I don't. I do most of my work from eight to noon.

Has all the success gone to his head? Well, no, not entirely. He recalls going to his local printer to collect a batch of new stationery, and being brought down to earth with a bang. 'What are you doing now that you have given up your insurance business?' the printer asked. 'Writing,' replied Clancy. 'Gee, where can I get your book?' The fact that *The Hunt For Red October* had been in the bestseller list for months seemed to have passed the printer by.

Dick Francis OBE

First of all, know your subject, what you are going to write about. Familiarise yourself with the subject. Do your research and get the facts right.

When you are writing, try to capture the reader immediately. End each chapter with a cliffhanger. Don't allow your reader to put the book down at that point and go to sleep. Make them want to start the next chapter.

As for style, don't worry about it. It isn't so much that authors choose the style, the style chooses the author. You can't do except what you can do. That is why some people can write and others can't.

Clive Cussler

Mayday! (Mediterranean Caper in the US), Iceberg, Raise The Titanic, Vixen 03, Night Probe, Pacific Vortex, Deep Six, Cyclops, Treasure, Inca Gold, Dragon, Sahara, Shock Wave, Sea Hunters, Golden Buddha and Lost City. Sales in excess of 125 million copies worldwide.

CLIVE CUSSLER'S STORYTELLING speciality is sub-aqua adventure, stories of unremitting pace, tension and technical know-how. Reading his novels, it is easy to believe that he is an experienced diver. He is just that but, perversely, he lives far from the sea in Arizona.

His career closely parallels those of other bestselling writers. Firstly, because he broke into writing from a full-time job (in advertising, in his case), then because he had written small pieces for a local newspaper, though he certainly wouldn't have called himself a full-time journalist.

An almost myopic determination to complete whatever has been started seems to be one trait that all top authors share. So where, I asked, did Clive attain his drive, and what did he think led him eventually to become an author?

During my schooldays I was good at English, but just lousy in science and algebra, and geometry and calculus were wholly beyond me. So I stared out the window and daydreamed.

My main love was archaeology. I could rattle off Egyptian dynasties like most boys can rattle off winners in a World Series. When I got to Pasadena College, I thought, hell, there's no money in archaeology, which is true, there isn't, so I switched to journalism.

I took typing, because in the senior years, we had a choice of subjects. As a friend of mine and I were big on automobiles, there was no need to take autoshop. I could weld and cope with most mechanical problems. I never cared for woodshop, so we got this bright idea to go with the women, and really meet some girls. So we took Home Economics and Typing. The girls there were often mad with us, because our cakes rose higher than theirs. I often look back on that and laugh, because I learned typing because of a love for women.

Journalism appealed to me, until a reporter came out to talk to us one day, and somebody asked him how much we can expect to make, and whatever it was, I was making more than that by working part-time in a grocery store. So then I began to think about business.

But first Cussler enlisted in the Air Force, where he worked as a flight engineer and mechanic. His service took him to Korea, and by the time he completed his duty, he had been promoted to sergeant. His tour of duty also took him to the Pacific, where he was based for a time in Hawaii. It seems that most ex-servicemen, when reminiscing about their overseas postings, give the impression that they had ample time to relax and enjoy their surroundings. In Clive's case, it was the sea that he turned to.

With a friend of mine, I bought what we think was the first aqualung in Honolulu in 1952. We just took it back to the base, pumped in about six-hundred pounds of air, strapped the thing on and ran into the water. No instructions at all. All this was well before formal training and related associations were formed, but I spent many hours exploring and making discoveries under water. It was all great fun.

Many ex-servicemen will also testify, however, that life can be very boring after the programmed activities of military life have come to an end. Clive not only experienced this boredom, he also lacked the necessary motivation and drive to establish a career for himself. He and his service comrade and diving buddy ran a gas station on the San Bernadino Freeway, just outside Los Angeles.

We had that for about three and a half years. I could write a book on that. If you talked about being robbed, held up, and had cars crashing into the station... there were accidents all the time!

During weekends, we had that urge to discover things and we used to tramp around the deserts of Southern California, looking for lost gold mines, ghost towns, anything we could drum up, and yes, we did have our moments.

Once we found an old airplane that had vanished in the war, with the bones of some fellow still there. It had come down in a gulley and never been found. Then we found the bones of an old miner, which the Sheriff's Department identified as a lost prospector from about 1926. And we found some artefacts from a colonists' expedition from Mexico of 1776. It was really all very fascinating, so I guess that's where I got the bug to look for anything that was missing.

After a while, though, I began to tire of the business. Then I saw this advertisement for a supermarket advertising manager. I went to see them and claimed I had lots of freelance experience, which wasn't true, I didn't know the first goddamned thing about it. When I got there, I was asked to lay out an advertisement, so I went down – I had a VW then – bought a newspaper and copied the general layout of some other supermarket ad.

I showed it to my interviewer, and he said, 'That's not very good.' 'Well, it's the best I can do on my lap in the VW.'

'In that case,' he said, 'it's pretty good,' and he hired me.

His initiation into journalism came when he did some freelance writing for the *Globe Pilot* in Costa Mesa, California. He supplied some recipes for a cookery column, but he also had fun writing a column about restaurants, calling himself the 'phantom diner'. His identity may have been a secret, but he was quite well paid for the pieces, about $100 a time, and, naturally, with a free meal included. It was a job that he took seriously for, as he readily admitted, he was in a position to ruin a restaurant.

From advertising groceries, he set up an advertising partnership with Leo Bestgen to form Bestgen and Cussler. It was, by American standards, a small agency, employing just two other people, and they specialised in newspaper, magazine and radio work, being too small for television contracts. No sooner had they become established than Clive announced that he wanted to move on to one of Hollywood's big-time agencies. He and Bestgen parted on very amicable terms, leaving him free to join D'Arcy Advertising in 1965 as copy director. There he put together copy for advertisements for Budweiser, Ajax detergents and General Tires. Creating winning storylines and catchy headlines, he was clearly talented. But like James Herbert, he found that life in advertising did not totally satisfy him. Married and with two children, he found that he became bored with time on his hands after the children had been put to bed. It was then that the idea of writing a book really germinated. So where and when did the confidence to start writing a novel come from?

I don't know that I even thought about whether I had the confidence, it never really entered into my mind. Nobody ever encouraged me, but coming from advertising, I looked at the problem from that angle first. What kind of book should I write? I didn't have that great American novel burning within me, or a story of great-uncle Harry who came across the prairie in a covered wagon.

I finally struck on the idea of a series, after I had studied all those series characters – James Bond, he was in his prime; Dean Martin as Matt Helm was a hit. Having never written a book before, I studied other authors, and their style and rationale. Once I'd created the concept, I just plugged on through until it was finished.

My first idea, which went into *Pacific Vortex*, was based on Fu Manchu, and my villain turned out to be a yellow-eyed big character who lived under the sea off Hawaii. Dirk Pitt was just a secondary protagonist at the time, and as the story unfolded, I killed off just about everybody but Pitt.

The next book, which was *Mayday!* in the UK, and *Mediterranean Caper* over here; Pitt just came in and took the whole book away. I never did go back to the evil villain.

But, you know, I was unlike many writers. If you talk to most new authors, they think their first story, or book, should be chiselled in marble, and they never can figure out why it never gets published. I didn't really have any misconceptions, I thought that I would, well, just give it a try. I'm fortunate in being one of those people who, whatever they start, are driven to finish it. Crossword puzzles, or writing a book, if I start, I finish.

I was between advertising jobs, and contemplating writing again, when my wife said, 'If you want to write stories about the sea, then why don't you take this job?' The pay was poor. In fact, I remember, it cut my salary by two-thirds, but it meant working in three or four different scuba-diving shops. I did the promotions and all kinds of fun stuff, but when business was slow, I would sit at a card-table in the back of the shop and that's where I wrote *Mediterranean Caper*. OK, we had *Pacific Vortex*, that wasn't getting anywhere, but I thought *Caper* was good enough to get published.

It was really a better book and I did have some
help. I went out to bone up on English versus
[as opposed to] creative writing. You know,
people always asked me, when I was young,
did I have a teacher who inspired me? I never
did, but I did have an excellent teacher on one
of those creative writing courses at Orange
Crest College. She did inspire me: her name is
Pat Kubick.

I remember the first time I took chapter one
along, it was a big breakthrough day, 'cause I had
never really talked to other writers, or anybody
else. If you've ever been to one of these creative
writing courses, you will know that you get up
and read your poem, article, or whatever, and
your classmates just go animalistic, and tear
everybody's efforts to pieces.

I've seen women go into sobbing fits because
somebody has criticised their work, and there
would almost be fights. We had this – oh she
really was an awful old lady – who would rip the
hell out of anybody who read out their work.
So I sat in fear when the first chapter of *Caper*
was read out, where the old plane appears and
strafes the modern American jet base. At the end
I thought, here it comes, but not one hand was
raised. As the teacher looked around, I thought,

I'm really in deep trouble now, she turned to the old bat and said, 'Don't even you have anything to say?' She looked up and said, 'No, it's good.' And I knew I had arrived.

So I finished *Caper*, and at this point I figured I needed an agent. I contacted some friends in Hollywood; I knew a lot of people in the public relations business, and they gave me names of literary agents in New York. I got devious at this point, so rather than just sitting down and writing the usual letter of query and the sample chapter, I went out and printed five hundred sheets of stationery and envelopes as the 'Charles Winthrop Agency'. I used to live on Winthrop Drive when I was a kid, and I always thought that it was a classy name.

I used my father's address in Laguna Hills and wrote to the first name on the list. He happened to be Peter Lampack, then a junior literary agent at the William Morris Agency. I wrote, 'Dear Peter, As you know I primarily handle motion-picture and television screenplays, but I've come across a couple of book-length manuscripts which I think have a great deal of potential. As you're aware, I'm retiring, would you like to take a look at them?' About ten days later, Dad says,

'There's a letter here from a man called Peter Lampack. Shall I read it to you?'

It read, 'Dear Charlie, Sure, if you say so. I'll take a look at the manuscripts.' So I mailed them off. A few days later another letter came. 'Dear Charlie, the first manuscript's pretty mediocre, the second one's pretty good. Where can I sign this guy Cussler?'

I almost fell off my chair! I fired off this letter, telling him where to find Clive Cussler, and he wrote introducing himself. He sent me his contracts, which I signed. That was 1969.

It wasn't easy to get a publisher. Peter never gave up, he struggled through 1970 and 1971, and in 1972, apparently, his boss said, 'Get rid of Cussler, he's not going anywhere.' Peter said 'No, I think he's got something,' and he finally got *Caper* placed with a small house. They published fifty-thousand copies and sold about thirty-two thousand. A year or two later, *Iceberg* came out and they paid me five-thousand-five-hundred bucks. Published five thousand copies and sold about three-thousand-five-hundred. Then came *Raise The Titanic*.

Cussler is a very determined man and, whether at work or at play, he applies the same dedication to the job in hand, as his hobby of hunting shipwrecks demonstrates. It is a pastime that combines his interest in archaeology with his passion for underwater adventure. When we met, he claimed to have found only nineteen wrecks, but press releases credit him with thirty-four historical findings, amongst which are two Civil War ships – the Union's *Cumberland*, and the Confederacy's *Florida*. Whenever he does locate a new wreck – and he has been seen searching the North Sea and around the coasts of Scotland, Denmark, Holland and France – he never claims salvage rights. His satisfaction lies in finding and identifying those wrecks. It is a costly business, upwards of £30,000 a trip, but thanks to his alter ego, Dirk Pitt, who has earned him millions of dollars, he can afford it.

When the typescript for Cussler's third novel, which he had simply entitled *Titanic*, was finished, Peter Lampack sent it to the publisher of *Mediterranean Caper* in the usual way. Sadly for the publishers, they turned it down on the grounds that 'it was a little too heavy, and paper costs have gone up.' Peter then sent it off to Putnam, who wanted a massive rewrite, which Clive refused to do. Then it was given to Viking, who took it on as it stood, paying him an advance of $7,500.

He still has that rejection slip. In the light of the book's huge success, it is more than an amusing memento; it is another bad dream for publishers who turn down typescripts which later turn out to be bestsellers.

The sinking of the RMS *Titanic* in 1912, with the loss of some 1,490 lives, is arguably the worst single peacetime shipping disaster in history. The disaster had a huge emotional impact on seagoing travellers, both at the time and afterwards. Several films, fictional and documentary, have been made, and many books published since the liner collided with an iceberg and sank, all fuelling the public's interest. By 1976 the disaster had become a legend; by then literally hundreds of thousands of people had heard about this ship.

Then, in 1976, a new book was published, apparently reviving the story. *Raise The Titanic* was just the story to entrance readers, because it was almost believable. (In some ways it presaged the work of Dr Robert Ballard who, in September 1985, actually located and filmed the wreck of the

Titanic, later publishing a vivid and evocative pictorial account, *The Discovery of the Titanic*.) Once Cussler's book had caught the public eye, sales soared, and its success increased the sales of his earlier novels.

One factor, perhaps, helped single him out for fame and fortune. Like Frederick Forsyth with his *The Day of the Jackal*, Cussler also used a true story as a basis for his fictional theme, a story of which there was already a firm awareness in the public's mind. A marketing person might say, albeit cynically, that the author wrote the story in order to take advantage of this wide readership base.

Publishers, writers, and booksellers might also say that had the novel been published simply as *Titanic*, the fortunes of Clive Cussler might have been very different. Between leaving its author and appearing in the bookshops, the title was changed. Several authors have confessed to being unable to think of catchy titles for their work – even ex-advertising people...

> Yes, I think my titles stink! I don't know what it is, I just can't title a book. It was the sales department [at Viking], when they were ready to do the jacket, who came back and suggested

that they could get more mileage out of *Raise The Titanic*. They were right.

Vixen 03 was a stupid title; I wish now, I'd named it *Quick Death* which was the nerve gas they used. *Mediterranean Caper* was a ghastly title; that was my first [published novel] so the editor picked it and I didn't argue. *Iceberg* was OK, *Cyclops* probably isn't too bad. *Treasure* is good.

When I think back to my days in advertising, when we really sweated on a headline, and the more money there was on the account the more we sweated, I feel guilty about titling. I know I could do better.

The action in all of Clive Cussler's books takes place in or around water, whether lake, river or ocean. His chief character and alter ego, Dirk Pitt, is very much a part of the magic formula that has made Clive's books so popular.

When he is writing, he disciplines himself to work rigid hours, knowing that authors must have that determination if they are ever to succeed. He works the same hours as he used to when he was in advertising: 'nine to five – with an hour off for a Martini.'

His first two books were written in the evenings and at weekends; he firmly believes that any ambitious author should begin by writing in his or her spare time. It seems only common sense to retain a full-time job, for writing is not an occupation from which anyone can immediately earn a living; indeed, only a small percentage of published writers actually pay the rent from their work. When Clive set out to write *Raise the Titanic* he was still employed full-time in advertising at Mefford, Wolff and Weir. Only after the huge success of that novel was he able to give up his job.

Clive sets himself a daily target, normally achieving about 1,000 words, roughly four pages. If he has a really good day and everything flows, he will achieve six pages, and if not, just two. Naturally, what he writes depends upon the thought and research he puts into a book, but these accrue over variable, and often very long, periods of time. When he has finished the typescript, he is ready to hand it over.

> Right from the beginning, I always stand or fall on the finished typescript. I have never sent a chapter out, or a summary. What the publisher gets, is what he gets.

These are sentiments with which many other authors would agree. However, it is all very well for an established and successful writer to make such statements, but a different matter for the novice.

Cussler's message for eager authors is somewhat unusual:

> My advice? Copy someone else! Find a successful author you idolise in the genre you are interested in and copy, not plagiarise the story, but the writing style. They don't seem to teach writing style on any courses that I have found, whether to use a prologue and epilogue, or whether you want to write in the first or third person, the benefits of flashbacks, or how to divide it into sections.
>
> I try to end a chapter with a hook. Like the old Saturday matinée serials. The reader will probably be in bed when he'll hit that point, but he'll always sneak a peek at the start of the next [chapter], then I'll hook him again. Writing a book is no different from an inventor inventing a product. You sit there and create this thing. . .

Arthur Hailey

1956, I think it was, I was thirty-six and had virtually given up hope of becoming a storyteller. I had mentally given up. I was doing quite well, relatively, in those days. My own small advertising and sales promotion business showed signs of expanding. And then, on a business flight from Vancouver, I dreamed up a play which became *Flight Into Danger*.

It was a totally uneventful flight, as I recall, except that the *North Star*, a DC4B, was the noisiest aircraft in the world. It had four engines which I'm pretty certain were Canadian. There was no way you could sleep and it was a long flight. I got tired of reading and just sat and daydreamed as a substitute for sleep. I guess I've always had that kind of mind. I have it now, because sometimes in bed, or in the shower, I think up a story situation.

I daydreamed a story, and the point was, at that time, 1956, I was a rusty old pilot. I had, during the war – flown and was competent to fly, but hadn't flown since 1947 when I came out of the RAF. I had never flown a four-engined airplane, though I had flown fast twin-engined

Beaufighters. I guess I asked myself, if anything could go wrong, could I fly this aircraft? In those days, you thought of it as an enormous thing to do.

Then, I suppose, one thought led to another and I asked myself, what would cause me to be required to fly it? It was a Friday night. I do remember that, and in those days, you had the choice of fish or meat as an in-flight meal. Catholics observed fish on Fridays, but I remember having meat. Suppose both pilots ate infected fish? Could I fly this aircraft? Would the stewardess be able to help me fly the aircraft? Would there be a doctor? I put the pieces together mentally because of those bloody noisy engines. If it hadn't been for them, I'd have probably gone to sleep.

When I arrived, I enthusiastically told Sheila [his wife] about my wonderful idea. She encouraged me, and I sat down to write it as a television play. [It took him less than ten days to finish it and the Canadian Broadcasting Company accepted it within two weeks. He wrote twelve television plays before a publisher asked if he'd write *Flight Into Danger* as a novel.]

He enjoyed three major worldwide successes with *Hotel*, *Airport* and *Wheels* (1965, 1968 and 1971 respectively), which were selected as *Reader's Digest* Condensed Books choices, and made into films. *Airport*, the film, had two sequels, *Airport '77* and *Airport '79*; *Airport*, the book, appeared in the *New York Times* bestseller list for 64 consecutive weeks, and for 30 of these at number one.

Publishers' motives for paying high advances can be whittled down to one: they are confident of achieving extremely high sales. They know, too, that such an author will back the publicity effort and take part in promotional tours and other activities, such as book-signing sessions and radio, television and newspaper interviews.

I take part for two reasons. One is that I feel an obligation to the publisher and to the salesman. I was a salesman once myself, and I like to share in that and make my contribution. The other is that after having spent three years on a book, it's exciting to come out in the open when the book is published and participate. Between books, I disappear from sight; I avoid publicity. There's no point in having publicity between books, which is why I never seek it out.

I think one of the reasons why I get attention when any of my books comes out is that I haven't been heard of since the last time. I don't get some literary agent to put my latest *bon mot* in the gossip columns, as I know some writers do.

I've found it easy to go on television and be relaxed. Not everyone does. When I go on television, radio, or even give a newspaper interview, I feel an obligation to them. I have made a commitment. They have given me some of their time. When I go on a show now, I usually submit a paper in advance, because there are so many books being published and the interviewer is very unlikely to have read yours. I list a summation of points that I can talk about if you want to bring them up. The one thing you must always do, is to make the interviewer look good. It isn't smart to score off the interviewer, and it helps you if you can help the interviewer.

If you can get into a news column for some reason, that's great. The difficult thing about any book is to make people aware that it exists, and that is the advantage of being on television.

What advice does he have for the aspiring author?

Get on with it. There are people who 'talk book', and there are people who 'write book'; talking writers, and writing writers.

Do what research you need to do. Some people don't need to research very much. Pay attention to every small detail because if a reader knows it is wrong, it will ruin the whole book for him.

It helps to be nosy. Read, read and keep reading. Remember, it's a very lonely life, writing.

Frederick Forsyth CBE

The Biafra Story, The Day of the Jackal, The Odessa File, The Shepherd, The Dogs of War, The Devil's Alternative, The Fourth Protocol, The Negotiator, The Deceiver, The Fist of God, Icon, Avenger and No Comebacks.

HIS MOTHER AND father were both shopkeepers in Ashford, Kent; his grandfather had served in the Royal Navy; his grandmother was a furrier in Gillingham; and his mother's father was a garage mechanic. It is hardly surprising, then, that writing was not one of his early ambitions.

When we met at his 190-acre farm in Hertfordshire, he reflected on his early aspirations.

As a schoolboy, his first ambition had been to fly but, more importantly, he developed a yearning to travel, to see the world. He explained that both ambitions originated from his home environment, where his imaginative mind had been fired by the places he had read about.

I was a voracious reader. Television, well, it had been invented, but we did not have one in our household. I think my parents got their first television when I was in my mid-teens, so my earlier years were spent reading books. Apart from the radio – then called the wireless – and the gramophone, one read. My parents were avid readers. So the three of us, in the evenings, would sit just reading.

I found I went through all the usual baby books. I skipped Beatrix Potter, but read a bit of Enid Blyton. Enjoyed the usual comics like *Beano* and *Dandy*, and later graduated to Richmal Crompton's *Just William* books.

But I was also interested in more adventurous stuff, and I recall taking individual authors and consuming everything that they ever wrote. I had my John Buchan period, and I read *The Dancing Floor*, *The Island of Sheep*, *The Three Hostages*, *Greenmantle*. I did not have a Henty period; I wasn't a great imperialist. Jeffery Farnol – now unknown. I liked the adventure stories about the old pirates and knights and what I suppose we call period-costume stuff. I just read a lot.

I also became fascinated by aeroplanes. I read all about the First World War fighter pilots: Bishop, McCudden, Mannock; and the Germans,

Immelman, Göring; and the French, Garros and Guynemer. I just became smitten with the idea that one day I was going to fly.

From the First War, I graduated to the Second World War, and read all the memoirs of Bader, 'Johnnie' Johnson and Pierre Clostermann. I consumed them all, one after the other. And I retained a lot, too: I have a good retentive memory. So, between adventure and flying, I suppose the only clue in that little boy in Ashford is that there was someone trying to get out and get away, and go places.

If the young Forsyth was bright and imaginative, he was not academic, though he developed a passion for languages and soon became competent in French and German, and, later, Spanish. Although he enjoyed languages, he made a conscious decision not to further his education by going on to university. He spent four years at Tonbridge School where he developed very strong views about the public school system.

I didn't like, or enjoy, the discipline, the hierarchy, the rigid and stratified chain of command that pertains in a public school. It didn't suit me. I was always a bit of a loner, and what with my head filled with fantasies of bullfighting and flying... At least, bullfighting after reading *Death in the Afternoon*, Ernest Hemingway's classic. Flying, for obvious reasons I've described.

There I was at Tonbridge, with a flair for languages and a profound yearning to get out and see the world. There's one other influence on that.

My father, in the after-war years, used to read every day the *Daily Express*, in the days when it was run by Beaverbrook and the editor, Art Christiansen. And they had in those days – they don't today – a bevy, a stable perhaps, of forty of the best foreign correspondents. Almost every day I would lean – and I'm talking about a nine- or ten-year-old – lean over my father's shoulder and read the headlines. Very often underneath would be 'Beirut', and then the date. I would ask my father where Beirut was, and he was enormously patient and helpful. Right, he would say, I'll show you. He would get the large school atlas out and tell me where Beirut was. Capital of the Lebanon, but he didn't just say it was there, and then go back to the paper. He told me about the Lebanon. He'd been through Port Said, he'd been to the Orient, had seen India, even planted rubber in Malaya. A much travelled man... I could probably name ninety per cent of the capitals of the world, because that's where the newspaper correspondents filed their reports from, and I just determined that, one day, I was going to get out of Ashford, and I was going to see them all.

So the wanderlust was born there. The desire to fly was born there; and the desire for exotica, for the sand and sun, and for the red colours of the bullring, were all born there, in that little house in Ashford.

Forsyth left school when only 'seventeen and four months' (he was very precise about that), with the immediate aim of doing his National Service in the Royal Air Force. Unlike many others he had some flying experience, having learned how to fly a Tiger Moth (a single-engined biplane).

I wasn't allowed to join the Air Force until I was seventeen and a half. Even then I snipped six months off the legal age of eighteen.

I started at Ternhill, in Shropshire, on an aircraft called a Provost, a Hunting-Percival Provost T1 trainer. It was a two-seater, side-by-side, with a fixed undercarriage. That took up nine months of

what's called basic flying, and then we went on to
an advanced flying training school at Worksop in
Nottinghamshire. That was on Vampires.

Not only did he see a good deal more of England
through his National Service, but also other parts of
Europe. He managed to hitch a seat on RAF flights
to Beirut, France, Germany, Gibraltar, Malta and
Spain. After leaving the RAF he secured a job on
a provincial newspaper, which scarcely seems the
best way of seeing the world, if that was his real
ambition.

I thought that, as I hadn't got enough money to
finance my own travelling, I would find a job that
enabled me to do it. That seemed to be a foreign
correspondent.

… So I enquired, how best to become a Fleet
Street correspondent, and I was told nobody
gets into Fleet Street straight from school, or
straight from National Service, you had got to
do your time first in a provincial newspaper. I
asked around, and consulted the editor of the
Ashford paper, the *Kentish Express*, and he was
a very nice guy. He took the magazine called
World Press News, which was the trade magazine

of journalism, which I borrowed, and in the Situations Vacant column I spotted an advert for a cub reporter on the *Eastern Daily Press*. I asked him about it and, he said, 'It's a very good paper, but it's a daily rather than a weekly, and most people start on a weekly paper. At least you'll soon learn the discipline of working for a daily paper, with six deadlines a week. If I were you, I'd write off for it.' Which I did, and got my interview in Norwich.

I was really very lucky, for the editor-in-chief was a man who had been a correspondent in the Spanish Civil War and was interested that I spoke French, German and Spanish. He took me on as a cub reporter, but the thing was, I had to sign a three year contract.

In May 1961 he moved to London, an experienced reporter in his early twenties. He joined Reuters, the world-famous news agency which has offices all over the world. It took him just eight months to fulfil his dreams.

The chance of a foreign posting was something most correspondents dreamed about. I was surrounded by people who were much older than I, and I was twenty-three then. Luck – I've had so much luck, so many flukes and coincidences that turn out right for me – a guy put his head around the door of the office one day and said, 'Anyone here speak French?' So I said, 'Yeah. Me.'

'Right,' he said, 'come with me.'

He took me off to the head of the French Desk, who was French, and said to this guy, 'See if this cub speaks French.' So the Frenchman turned to me, and rattled off several sentences in French and I rattled off several sentences back in French. He was a busy man, in shirtsleeves, with bands to hold his sleeves up, tapping away upon his typewriter (we didn't have computers in those days), and he just looked up, and said, 'Hee speekes vair good French. Why?' So then the other fellow who had summoned me said, to him, not me, 'The Deputy Editor, Paris, has got a heart murmur, and he's going to have to be flown home. They are screaming for a replacement.' So the Frenchman said, 'We-ell, send 'eem. E's all right.' And that was it. I was on.

'When can you leave?'

'Instantly!' I said, 'tonight.' I only had a bedsitter and an MG sports car. No real ties, one suitcase held all my belongings. I garaged the car, paid up the rent on the flat to the end of the week, and I was on the evening plane to Paris.

And that was May 1962, during the height of the OAS crisis, with Algeria due for her independence on 1 July. Assassination attempts were being hatched against [President] Charles de Gaulle, and the Foreign Legion had gone into mutiny along with the 11th Colonial Paras, the crack French regiment in Algeria.

I met the French bodyguard around de Gaulle, because I was, as the cub reporter, the youngest, the junior, and given what was deemed to be the most boring job, which was following de Gaulle around… Not because what he was doing was of enormous interest, but in case he suddenly went down with a bullet through his head. Here was a kind of Kennedy assassination that was foreseen, that was awaited on an hourly basis. … Well, in the periods between when he moved in his guarded limousine came the waiting, which every journalist will tell you is part of the job. You wait, and you wait, and you wait. The British, American, Swedish, Danish, Finnish and Norwegian press corps kept themselves to themselves in a single group, and the French in the other. I, because I was bilingual, joined the French group, and there I got to know and listened to the reminiscences of the bodyguards and drivers, and later, when I needed it, I could always call on these contacts, calling in markers, because I'd done favours for them, and they would talk to me about what it was really like to try and protect that man. That is why the authenticity of *The Day of the Jackal* is genuine.

I also knew bars where I could find OAS sympathisers, and because I was curious – not because it made a story, but because I was curious – I would frequent them. I would listen to their side, of how the great traitor de Gaulle had given Algeria away to the wogs, and so on. These were the OAS, the ultra-rights. As a journalist, I found I could move between all segments of society, from high society, the diplomats and politicians, to the underworld, the rebels, and the security service, counter-intelligence, and, amongst them, killers.

Forsyth's career as a diplomatic correspondent for the BBC is another reason why he was able to use his investigative experience as a base for the thrillers he was destined to write. It must be said, however, that just being a journalist and mastering the art of gathering information is not an automatic passport to becoming a bestselling writer.

However, when he became a freelance correspondent working in Biafra, he was greatly moved by the many children he saw dying as a result of the war and, knowing that the British government of the day supported the oppressors (France, by contrast, supported the Biafrans), he felt compelled to put all that he had seen and learned into a book.

Back in London on leave, he just happened to saunter down to his local pub, the Mason's Arms in Devonshire Street, where he liked to enjoy a drink and the convivial conversation of acquaintances. Among the friends there was one Brian Seaton-Hunt.

> We got talking and he mentioned that he was an agent, albeit in a small way. I said, 'Well, I'm an author in a very small way.' He asked, 'What have you written?', and I told him that I had just finished a manuscript about Biafra.
>
> Now, the serendipity of the whole thing is that barely a week earlier, he had been talking to Rob Hutchinson [the editor for Penguin's Africa list] who had told him, 'We really could use a book about Biafra as a Penguin Special'. And so

> obviously Brian Seaton-Hunt said to me, 'I think I
> know how it can be placed', but he didn't tell me
> about Rob Hutchinson then. But he said, 'Give
> me the manuscript.' I did. And he took it to Rob,
> who said to Brian, 'This is exactly what we are
> looking for. Good controversy about Biafra.'

Penguin did indeed publish his non-fiction book
about Biafra, though he never saw the proofs or
cover designs because by the time the book was in
production he was back in Nigeria. He was paid an
advance of just £50 for *The Biafra Story*, against
a royalty of about 3d (1.25p) per copy. Despite
this seemingly small sum, he earned some £350
in all, for the publishers sold the entire run of
30,000 copies.

Most authors whose first book had sold that
number of copies would be tempted to continue in
the genre that had brought them success. Forsyth,
however, like Barbara Taylor Bradford, believed he
could write other subjects.

> I found myself, in January 1970, back in this
> country from the Biafra War, without a contract
> or a commission, freelance, and therefore

unemployed. I was like an actor 'resting', with time to kill, no income coming in, and not much in the bank. I had an idea in my head. I had mulled it over for some six years, from the time I had been covering the OAS attempts to assassinate Charles de Gaulle in Paris.

...I had picked so many trashy paperback pseudo thriller novels off airline bookstalls, and after a hundred pages in the middle of a flight, closed them and said, 'This is absolute nonsense. The man does not even know what he is talking about. He hasn't even made an attempt to know what he's talking about.' And that irritated me.

... I had a conviction that if I couldn't do better, at least I could do as well.

I felt that if one was going to write a thriller, one ought to make it credible. And credibility, it seems to me, is about getting the facts right, especially where you were going into facts rather than fiction.

So I did just that. I wrote what turned out to be *The Day of the Jackal* without a contract, and [without a] publisher, in thirty-five days in January and February [1970]. And without a clue as to how to get a novel published.

With the novel finished, the first person he went to, of course, was his drinking companion, and agent, Brian.

> I really didn't know how it was done. A year later, I had this much bigger typescript, and a thriller novel to boot, and no idea what one does about getting a book published. Who do you go to? Who do you see? I soon discovered that it was a 'catch twenty-two'. If you are a big and popular novelist, you have no trouble getting a top agent. A top agent will have no trouble getting you published. But if you are a 'who's he?' nonentity, with an unpublished manuscript, and a first to boot, then the big blue-chip agents don't want to know.
>
> My work was submitted in sequence to four publishers: W. H. Allen, Cassell, Collins, and then Michael Joseph.
>
> I got rejection slips from the first, second, and third. It was with Michael Joseph for about eight weeks, from mid-July to mid-September, and I hadn't had a word back. It was frustrating, but it was the holiday period, and quite coincidentally – well, not quite – I did actually do a bit of beavering myself. I met [the late] Harold Harris,

who was then editorial director of Hutchinson – oddly enough, in the same bar at the Mason's Arms.

It so happened that Hutchinson then were right across the other side of Great Portland Street [i.e. near the pub], and Harold Harris had dropped in for a beer. Brian introduced me to him, but nothing much came of it. The book was not even mentioned, but I had already by then decided that Brian was getting nowhere, and I thought – wrongly or rightly, whatever – the reason he was getting nowhere was that nobody was reading the damn thing. I didn't think it was that bad…

What I'll do, I thought, is write a synopsis. So I wrote the synopsis, which covered all the twenty-four chapters in the book in one page per chapter. After that was done, I went back to Hutchinson and I inveigled myself into the presence of Harold Harris, and I said, 'I've got this typescript.' His eyes glazed over, you know, in a sort of disbelief; after all, he was a busy man and had rank after rank of secretaries to protect him from unsolicited typescripts. But being a very courteous man he said, 'I see.' Then I cantered on, saying, 'I don't want you to read the typescript, it's too long, it'll take you for ever.

But would you read the synopsis?'

After twenty minutes he looked up [from the synopsis], and said, 'It could be interesting, where is it?' I replied, truthfully, 'It is with Michael Joseph.' He stared at the ceiling for some time and he said, 'It is absolutely out of the question for me to examine a typescript that is in the hands of another publisher. Good day.'

But I read the body language, went outside, got a cab, and went down to Michael Joseph, though by this time it was the lunch hour. I asked at reception for it back, and a junior duly gave it to me. He said, 'Are you formally withdrawing it?' I said, 'Yes I am.' And without any more ado, they gave it to me, the whole typescript, with elastic bands in two directions to hold it together. I literally shoved it under my arm and went back to Great Portland Street, where I gave it to Harold Harris, less than thirty minutes after leaving him.

This was the Friday, and on Monday Harris called me up and said, 'If you'll be here at four p.m. with your agent, we'll discuss a contract.'

So I called Brian and told him the news and we duly presented ourselves at four p.m. The most interesting thing about all this was that Harold Harris suggested that I sign what's called a three-novel contract. The question then arose, and it arose before I left the office, 'Do you have any ideas for a successor [book]?'

Bold as brass I said, 'Yes, of course I have, scores of ideas, and just as intriguing as this one,' but actually I hadn't an idea in my head. So I went away, literally to think up another theme.

From then on, I was devoting a lot of time trying to think up another theme. And I came up with two. One based on the notion of hunting a missing Nazi; some shades, if you like, of the Eichmann hunt, which had taken place ten years earlier in 1960, and with some shades of Nazi trials that had taken place at that time.

The alternative was a novel based on mercenaries in West Africa. So I wrote up the general idea, on one page, and in the broadest possible brush strokes. Then, about a fortnight later, I went back to Harold Harris and said, 'Which one would you prefer?'

Unhesitating, he chose the Nazi one, which came to be known as *The Odessa File*.

Had he, I wondered, ever tried to analyse why *The Day of the Jackal* was so popular?

I think there are three things that intrigue.

One, and this sounds very big-headed, but it is very basic, you must have a story to tell. You can't take an episode and spin it out for four hundred pages. You can't take one single rather smart idea, and pad it to a blockbuster. The story must be a pretty big story in itself.

I would say you've got to have what you reckon is a cracker of a story. The idea of knocking off the president is, you know, a fairly big issue, assassinating presidents is big enough for people to say, yes, I believe all this effort would probably go into trying to prevent it. Whereas all that effort might not go into trying to prevent an offence against, say, the Litter Act.

The second one – and this people said to me later – it is all innovative, it's never been done before.

I don't know why, but I'm rather a stickler for accuracy. It seemed to me, as a reader, that I was interested in how things worked, how things were done, what the procedures were. I would find it unsatisfying, as a reader, if this bank clerk suddenly whips out a loaded gun, because by and large bank clerks do not have loaded guns and your ordinary chap on the Penge eight-forty-nine a.m. to Cannon Street, or wherever, is going to be pretty hard put to go and get a Colt forty-five. There has to be procedure: how on earth did he get the damn thing? And when people produce these marvellous high tensile sets of burglar tools, I'm intrigued to know where they get them from. So, I thought, if you are going to start talking about false passports, let's find out how you get false passports. So I found a professional forger, and he told me. He was rather displeased later when it all appeared in print, because he said, 'I do have a wife and children to support, and now every punter is going to be doing it.'

I said there are three things that intrigue. The third is that the readers like being taken behind the scenes. I liken it to a stage. Most of us sit watching the television or reading the newspapers, as the audience to a production. We see the ministers on their best behaviour, and we see the civil servants at their most urbane. I take them back and show them the actors without their make-up on. I explain what goes on behind the façade that the captains of industry, politics, senior civil service and military defence show us. The readers seem to think there's something behind the headline, and I'm going to tell you what really happened and which wasn't in the papers.

So, accepting that he is able to procure accurate and detailed information from his special sources, does he really believe that it is just attention to detail that ensures his novels become bestsellers? Is that aspect more important to the success of his books than, say word of mouth, publicity, or advertising?

> That's a good one. If publishers could answer that, they would know exactly where to spend their budgets, and none of them can. *Jackal* was clearly word of mouth, by the fact of its having a launch print of eight thousand copies. It wasn't necessarily the sort of book that every reviewer will jump at like the next le Carré, or the next Jeffrey Archer.
>
> I think that word of mouth was undoubtedly to a large degree the main reason. Later, yes, of course, there was a publicity budget and yes, there were reviews and there were interviews, and promotional campaigns, and advertising books on television like any other product. Like cornflakes!
>
> Then you've got paid and unpaid promotion; permeation chat shows on radio or television, like *Start the Week*. It suits the journalist, because he's got a personality on his show, it suits the

publisher because he's got his author on the show. It probably suits the author because it may raise his royalties. Then you've got all the paid, purely paid, promotional publicity.

Fortunately, at the merest rumour of another Forsyth thriller, orders start to arrive at the publisher's sales office, but he accepts that all that might change one day.

Oh, the fickleness of the public. I can't predict what they want next year, and I don't think anybody can… Everyone's looking for a winning formula, film makers are, novelists are; all I can do is to devise an idea that interests me. If it doesn't interest me, I won't do it anyway because I can't sustain the interest to do it.

Joseph Wambaugh

It wasn't something that you talked about to other policemen, and it wasn't something that any policeman ordinarily does. If they knew I was going to college, I would pretend, if anyone asked me, to be studying law, police science or criminology. I think I was the only serving officer studying literature. I wasn't afraid of being teased, but I did not want to appear different from the others. I certainly didn't mention I was trying to write. I was a closet writer.

Having got my degree, I did not tell anybody at work. I started fooling around writing short stories, because everybody on the face of the earth who has ever majored in English tries to write, whether he admits it or not. And you know, they all say they don't, but they do. Anyway, I was one who did and I just sent them to magazines; little short stories about police work, you know, but they were all rejected. In fact, I recall that *Playboy* magazine even sent a mean little note with one of them saying, 'This is the second time you've sent the same story to us, schmuck. Don't do it again, it's no better this time than it was last time.'

I always regretted that I didn't hang on to that letter because some years later, *Playboy* was trying to get me to do a piece for them and I would have loved to have sent it back to them in revenge.

The publishing game is old-fashioned, and the marketing is years behind the times. No one takes a great deal of trouble to find out why people read books, why they buy certain books.

I wonder why a publisher doesn't just bite the bullet and spend several thousand dollars for a very good marketing survey – not just on one book, let's say on thirty books and, let's say, share the cost with other publishers; to find out why some books are bought and others not. But they never do things like that, and so it's still an old-fashioned industry.

Robert Ludlum

What I try to do, and it is something everyone in the theatre knows, is [ensure] that the structure of a book is nothing more than the evolvement of one situation into another until there is a climax, with each segment being indispensable because, as with an audience, if you don't want to know what's happening from scene two, or from act one to act two, you're going to leave the theatre… I think it's all suspense and 'what-happens-next'.

My first editor, Richard Marek was most helpful as an editor, of course, and a writer who doesn't ask the advice of an editor is a fool.

I think word of mouth has helped me most, but then luck, timing and a fine agent help too. I think I've had publishers, especially my current publishers, who care, and they know how to market a book. That's important, too.

I think that developing a style and maintaining it by consistency and frequency of product helps, but [so too does] avoiding that fine line between under – and over – exposure, too many books too rapidly, because this generally leads to sloppy or unthoughtout work. This diminishes the consistency of style.

Then I don't describe sex scenes either, and that may help sales. To me, I think that it's much nicer, and much more evocative sensually, to use certain catchphrases, and to allude to certain things that we all know, to arouse an imagination but not to become prurient.

Every author, of course, has a 'beginning'.

It starts with someone in the world of publishing believing in, or at least liking, your work. In my case, it happened to be an agent, the same agent I've had all my life. It might also be an editor, invariably a hungry junior editor, anxious to make his mark by 'discovering' new talent; also because senior editors rarely have the time to pore over the voluminous new material submitted. Remember, senior editors were once junior editors.

Craig Thomas

Rat Trap, Firefox, Wolfsbane, Snow Falcon, Moscow 5000, Emerald Decision, Sea Leopard, Jade Tiger, Firefox Down, The Bear's Tears, Winter Hawk, All The Grey Cats, The Last Raven, A Hooded Crow, Playing With Cobras, A Wild Justice, A Different War. Worldwide sales of more than 20 million copies.

CRAIG THOMAS IS one of Britain's own master thriller writers. Born in Wales, Craig Thomas went to the University College, Cardiff, to read English, a subject at which he was to excel. With an MA degree behind him and a yen to continue in the world of education, he became a teacher, ending up at Shire Oak School in Walsall, in what was then the English county of Staffordshire.

He describes himself as the 'boy from Hicksville' who made good, and admits to being somewhat temperamental, impatient and emotional. Exceptionally hard-working – 'a dedicated workaholic' in his own words – he is mercurial but sensitive by nature. He too, like so many others, once daydreamed of becoming a writer, although not as a novelist, but as a radio or television playwright. Over a period of several years, he bombarded the BBC Script Unit with a variety of ideas, including a science-fiction serial and a radio version of part of J.R.R. Tolkien's *The Lord of the Rings*. Each time his submissions were returned, usually with a curt and impersonal rejection slip, until he thought, like thousands of writers in the same situation, that he was attempting the impossible. He had, too, also entered a number of writing competitions, but always to no avail.

His pride was undoubtedly dented by every returned script, but perhaps his training as a teacher guided him because, faced with these constant rejections, he sought advice. This is something that perhaps anyone might eventually have done, but the important factor in his case was that he asked one of the BBC script editors what he was doing wrong – could the editor advise him? Amazingly, this simple piece of lateral thinking helped put him on the road to fame. There seems little doubt that Craig could have gone on writing little pieces, gone on fruitlessly submitting scripts to the BBC, for many years, but for that singularly important advice.

The script editor's advice was gloriously simple: what Craig was writing was unsuitable for broadcasting. He ought to apply his talents to novels.

> Most of my efforts went to the BBC, a couple to ITV, but this was a part-time hobby rather than an occupation, and with unsolicited material for radio, you need the cast of characters, the summary of the plot, the sound effects, and so on, and samples of dialogue. So I spent vast amounts of time planning and structuring, and working out the material, but only as much time writing it as it took to have enough material to submit in the first instance. So it was that kind of hobby, instead of gardening, or keeping tropical fish, or do-it-yourself.
>
> In a way, going to the comprehensive [school, i.e. Shire Oak] and becoming a head of department, with the extra administrative and disciplinary work, drained me far more than expected, both physically and nervously. Intellectually, I was less stimulated, and less used up, and I think that, probably, I needed that kind of environment, with a certain amount of creative energy left over, to actually get a novel written.

Craig spent the next eighteen months writing his first novel. Once he had proved he could write a 350-page typescript, he put it to one side and started another, this time finishing it in just six months: it was published as *Rat Trap*.

For those who try, who have the energy and drive to get up and do something about their ambitions, life has a curious way of sometimes providing opportunities. So it was with Craig. Working hard at the school in Staffordshire precluded him from easy contacts – especially personal contacts – with publishers in London. It happened, however, that his father, Brinley Thomas, a long-serving journalist with the *Western Mail*, had had fifteen books published, and was therefore a notable author in his own right. These were all about rugby football, a far cry from fiction, but contacts are contacts, and Craig reckoned that his father simply must, by that time, know something about publishing, and whom to contact.

One of the publishing world's well-known personalities of the time, Bill Luscombe, had published his father's books, though he had, by then, left to join another London publisher. However, his 'little black book' of contacts was very wide-ranging, and he knew instantly whom to put Craig in touch with.

> I never actually met Bill, and having written *Rat Trap*, I asked if he knew anybody who would look at it – and tell me what they thought of it. Though I wasn't nervous of submitting *Rat Trap*, I knew it was better than my first attempt. Bill wrote a lovely letter back saying, 'Send it to Anthea Joseph, don't send it to Michael Joseph Ltd. Send it to Anthea personally. And enclose a copy of my letter.' Which I did.
>
> I realise now, with hindsight, how important that introduction was...

It was early in May 1975 when Craig sent his first typescript off to Anthea Joseph. For him it was a major breakthrough, because she replied on 11 June, saying, 'subject to you agreeing to some cutting and amendments, we should be glad to make you an offer.' After all those rejections, her letter became one of his most treasured possessions, a milestone in his life. She invited Craig to visit her in London, to discuss his first novel. On the day, he donned his best suit, a 'CIA-style' cream outfit, and headed off to meet Anthea. He vividly remembers the first time they met, for she took him to a little Greek restaurant just off Tottenham Court Road. Later on, after lunch, they went back to her office, where she introduced Craig to a colleague, Jenny Dereham, the editor who was to look after his work.

Was there no question of any literary agent being involved at this stage?'

Well, soon after this – yes. When *Rat Trap* was published, Mike Shaw of Curtis Brown, who had joined them a year before, wrote to me saying, 'I've just read your book with a great deal of interest. I think you could be very successful. But you need an agent. Could I come up and talk to you?'

So I had to take a long lunch hour from Shire Oak to take him to the local pub. I don't think he was awfully impressed with the meal, but he persisted with me, and the only reason I went to an agent was because I thought, nothing ventured, nothing gained. The week before, Jenny [Dereham] had telephoned me – and she's not daft, is our Jenny – she rang me up during a break in school and offered me one thousand pounds for *Firefox*, twice the money. [*Rat Trap* brought him an advance of £500.] 'Make your mind up now' – and I'm standing there waiting for the bell to go... 'Oooh, oooh, right, yes, that's wonderful. Thank you.'

If I had to do it again, I would have gone to an agent to begin with, rather than submit things to a junk-pile. I was lucky to avoid the junk-pile, but if it had been a junk-pile submission, then an agent is going to be of greater help. The fact of life is, because publishing is such a personal business, and the relations between publishers and authors are so personal, it is probably better to have an agent simply because somebody else talks about the vulgar subject of money.

At the time, he felt on top of the world with his advance of £500 in his pocket – not much by today's standards, perhaps, but this was 1975, well before the age of massive advances and publicity hype.

The money allowed me to give up those time-consuming evening classes, where I taught A-level English for two hours a week. My fellow teachers were very good about the whole thing, but I used to say to the inquisitive, 'Well, I'm trying to write a novel.'

'Oh,' they'd say, and they would go away, but there were no silly comments. They were even very tolerant, when they discovered I was leaving [the school] because the Americans had paid a lot of money for the paperback edition of *Firefox*. At times they were certainly curious. In fact, with *Firefox*, the geography staff were very good at helping me with the background about climatic conditions and the ice-floe [crucial to the plot]...

A most innovative thriller in its day, *Firefox* caught the eye of American publishers, and it was the sale of the US paperback rights in that novel which earned him enough to enable him to take the plunge and 'retire' from teaching.

There are a number of innovative aspects about *Firefox*, but basically, I wrote it because it seemed like a good idea at the time. Nobody had written a flying novel for years, especially a flying thriller; and nobody had used a Vietnam veteran in a thriller, and that was purely accidental, because I needed somebody who had flown in combat in the late seventies and therefore had to be a Vietnam veteran; and lastly, which I adopted from one unsubmitted novel, was the fact that it is the first thriller set (at least for half its length) inside the Soviet Union, in Moscow.

Those elements attracted both Michael Joseph and Sphere [the British paperback publishers]; especially Sphere... They had been looking for a home-grown bestselling thriller writer, and they'd found somebody who had one book published, and they knew that *Wolfsbane* [his third novel] had been finished by then. They had found an author who had written a novel different enough to be attractive on a wide scale...

It's an extremely simple structure which, put simply, is a chase from chapter one to chapter ten.

So that even if you are not going to be terribly interested in the Moscow background or the flying, you can be interested in the fact that a man is being chased for his life from start to finish. Literally from start to finish.

I remember talking to Anthea... on the first occasion we met, and she said the 'word-of-mouth' aspect was not that important; she didn't know how important it was, though it obviously was important. I'm sure word-of-mouth recommendation is the substance of a bestselling status. I think it has to be – this element of a loyal readership which creeps in more and more with each succeeding book.

They can ruin you in the same way. This far on in my career, it would take two or three awful books to finish me off, but they could finish me off.

The word certainly spread. *Firefox* went on to sell a quarter of a million paperbacks in the UK during the first twelve months of publication, and two million in the US.

I wondered, however, whether he agreed with others that excelling at English was a prerequisite for successful authors?

No, not at all. But I do think that I have probably learned something, whatever it is – and I wouldn't know what it is – from every book I've ever read. And I think that my grounding in and passion for English literature and the language make me a better writer in my genre than most of my peers.

But I don't think that it [command of English] is even the beginning of producing a novel. It certainly wouldn't produce a bestseller, or even a literary bestseller.

By 1978, when *Wolfsbane* was published, he was well and truly established as a full-time writer. His teaching days were now history, and with three books behind him he became totally dedicated to writing.

What about reviews? Did he get many for *Rat Trap*, or *Firefox*?

> I got a few, but, generally, I'm not an author who gets many reviews.
>
> I got a good one [for *Rat Trap*] in *The Times*, and a good one in *The Guardian*, and a couple of other smaller reviews. For *Firefox*, I got a reasonable one in *The Times*, but I didn't get one in *The Guardian*, and I got a fair number in regional papers. And then I suppose my review status went down and down and down, until *The Bear's Tears*, [which] got very good reviews from a number of newspapers. But I long ago learned not to expect much.
>
> I do, however, get good reviews in America. Especially for *The Bear's Tears*, which up until *All The Grey Cats*, is the book I've been proudest of. I got superb reviews in the *New York Times*, the *Washington Post*, and the *Wall Street Journal*. And I thought, yes, thank you. They were lengthy and

> detailed, but I got a terrible review for *Winter Hawk* in the *Boston Globe*.

At this point Craig's wife, Jill, remarked with a good deal of feeling that they both resent reviews in which it is clear that the writer has not read the book in question. This is a view held by all writers, whether bestsellers or not; besides, such reviewers manage only to diminish their own credibility.

Authors are no different from anyone else: any criticism can hurt them. Everyone likes to be praised and good reviews are like gold; conversely, bad reviews can be very painful. Some writers pay no attention to reviews at all, others, at least early on in their careers, sneak glimpses and, if they are good, read on.

I told Craig that one of the authors I interviewed, Barbara Taylor Bradford, had said, with considerable truth, that 'writing cannot be taught, but it can be learned.'

> Now that's not a bad comment. I think the passion for language cannot be born, it can only be acquired, because you don't have any language when you are born. But there is something

similar to the quality that makes a mathematician, or a musician-stroke-composer, that produces that passion for language, which is the first way in which you are going to write, without knowing anything about characterisation, dialogue, and those adult things. The childish thing about writing is the language, the words. And that is acquired as early as Mozart was composing his first concertos, and so on. You acquire it when you learn to read.

Jill Thomas is now his trusted 'first editor'. Most authors, whether aspiring or established, like to get a reader's opinion before pressing on to the next chapter or section. In Craig's case, Jill had little to do with his work at first, but, as she explained:

The reason it started was because he had a chum, John Knowler, and he was English but he worked for an American publisher. He was an extremely perceptive man, and he was the one person who could really make Craig do exactly as he wanted him to with his editing. He was very sensitive, and very good, too. He used to say things like 'This is very good, but let's make it better.' Not just that, but his comments were encouraging, too: 'I can also recommend...' as a note in the margin; 'We are being told something here, but you are getting a piece of information across, and it is coming across as a piece of information rather than part of the story,' which made Craig, in turn, think and do it a different way.

Well, he died, and he was one of those people we were extremely fond of, and I said to Craig, 'Would you like me to just read it through and see what I think as a second opinion, before it goes in to the agent and publisher?' It sort of went on from there. And I've got worse and worse, and harder and harder.

And Craig added: 'It allows us, when we send the book in, to defend it, doesn't it?'

I doubt very much whether he has to defend his work nowadays. His days of £500 advances must seem like aeons ago; today, he is offered six figure sums just to clinch a deal. This is good money for doing something that he always wanted to do, but to win this level of reward he has to be a workaholic. He now works for six to eight months just researching his next book, then spends approximately the same time writing it. His working day starts at 9.30 a.m. through to 5.00 p.m., only allowing himself one coffee break in the morning and just half an hour for lunch.

It is clear from the interviews in this book that the life of a full-time writer is a very lonely one indeed. Authors who write from home, and most do, become virtual recluses, and it becomes very difficult for them to persuade friends and relatives that they really are working, and are not to be disturbed.

> We realised about five or six years ago that we were becoming a bit hermit-like. Reclusive. When people rang the doorbell at any time during the day, we kept saying 'Oh God, who's that?' instead of, 'Oh, I wonder who is at the door?' But we are more available nowadays.

One quality common to all the successful authors in this book is the attention they devote to detail; indeed, it seems that detail is critical to their success. This may seem obvious, but it is a common denominator among them. Many authors, Craig included, use cross-cutting (a technique of shifting between scenes, characters, action sequences, locations, time-frames, and back again) as a means of capturing and holding a reader's attention. It is an art that requires more planning, and more attention to detail, than a straightforward text. How does Craig cope?

I do plan with great care now, but I didn't in the early days.

The best story I can tell you about cross-cutting, as an instinctive art as opposed to a planned art – because I do plan my scenes, and I know what what's going to be in them, but I never plan where precisely, where they finish and the next one begins – [is about] when I was proof-reading *Firefox*. I got to the scene towards the end of the first half, where he [the central character] actually steals the plane. Now he is having one of his funny turns, his delayed stress [from Vietnam], he's having one of his turns while hiding in the pilots' restrooms, and I cross-cut it to that point in the hangar where they [dissidents helping with the theft] start the fire on the second prototype. Then cross-cut back to him, and as I was reading the proofs, I said, 'Oh God, I've got this wrong, come on, come on, it's taking too long, it's taking too long. And because I was saying it, I realised I hadn't got it wrong, it was right, because the reader is going 'come on, come on.'

That was the one piece in the film that wasn't exploited, the cross-cutting between those two [scenes]. In the film, the fire was more or less out and he just walked in, whereas in the book this useless individual who is supposed to be such a sky-hot pilot can't even get himself dressed in his flying suit.

Firefox, as it turned out, starred Clint Eastwood, who not only played the lead, but produced and directed as well. Perhaps that was the reason why Warner Brothers' representative had declined to break the news when the contract for the film rights was signed. Hollywood's hard man must have thought very highly of Craig's work, but how had Eastwood discovered the novel?

What he told me – so therefore it must be true – is not the often misquoted story that he picked up a copy from a bookstall at Heathrow.

I gather what happened was [that] a friend of his [who] runs a small private airline in Southern California... read it when it came out in paperback in the States, and gave Eastwood his copy, saying, 'Read it, you'll be great in the movie.' So he actually read the book, rather than a screenplay, which is quite unusual.

Firefox was a highly successful film, and it is almost a racing certainty that most of the audience thought that the scenes in Moscow were for real. In fact, all the 'Russian' scenes were filmed in Vienna and elsewhere in Austria. Perhaps what is more surprising, though, is that Craig Thomas never visited Moscow during the course of his research for the novel.

Looking back, and with the benefit of hindsight, what advice would he offer to someone contemplating writing a thriller?

Persistence. The virtue of persistence. Nothing else, because I can't say, not having met them, whether they have got talent, the facility, imagination, strength of character. But I do know they have to have persistence, and that can apply to anybody.

I always remember those old orange and white Penguins, and the exotic authors they had. They'd always been lumberjacks, brain surgeons, or beachcombers before they became authors. And that there was a syndrome whereby you had to experience everything before you wrote – usually – very bad books.

I would think that today's writer draws more consistently upon his imagination than upon his experience. I mean – it's no good being a monk unless you are writing a religious poem or novel, but other than that, I don't see that there's an apprenticeship to be served in the world before you can become a writer.

Afterword

READING ABOUT THE lives of these bestselling authors, their backgrounds, education and upbringing, it is possible to discern a loose pattern which provides a clue to success: an affinity for English, for reading, for storytelling, for fact-finding, and, above all, for being both imaginative and original. Each reader will, I hope, have found help here, and perhaps the inspiration to pursue their dreams. For others, those who just enjoy reading and not writing, I hope they have had their interest held, and have been intrigued by the authors' own tales of their journeys along the road to bestsellerdom.

Acknowledgements

FIRST AND FOREMOST, I am extremely grateful to all the authors interviewed for this book. They gave up their valuable writing time to talk about the subject for this book and their contributions will forever be a source of great interest.

In addition to the personal information given by authors, other references were drawn upon for background material, and I readily acknowledge the help of the following sources:

The Writer's Handbook for Ruth Rendell's quotation, reprinted by permission, from 'How Do You Learn to Write?' by Ruth Rendell, which appeared in *The Writer's Handbook* copyright © 1988 by The Writer, Inc., Boston USA.

The Writer's Handbook for Samm Sinclair Baker's quotation reprinted by permission, from 'Where to Sell: A 3 Point Checklist That Works' by Samm Sinclair Baker, which appeared in *The Writer's Handbook*, copyright © 1988 by The Writer, Inc., Boston USA.

Michael Joseph Ltd for an extract from Dora Saint's contribution in *At The Sign of the Mermaid* published in 1986. 'Miss Read' novels are published by Michael Joseph in hardback and Penguin in paperback.

H. F. Ellis for an appreciation of Dora Saint published in *The Sunday Telegraph*, February 1978.

Hugh Joseph for quotations from Anthea Joseph's letters, and article.

To my Elizabeth, whose patience I have stretched to the limit with my incessant questions and requests for an opinion.

Other sources acknowledged for assistance in the research of this book:

The Naval Institute Press

Sunday Express

The Sunday Telegraph

The Bookseller

The British Horse Society

Daily Express

David Higham Associates Limited

Ian Roberts and not least, the helpful staff of the Basingstoke Public Library.

ALSO AVAILABLE

How to get Published
Secrets from the Inside
Stewart Ferris

The concept that a good book will always find a publisher is outdated and over-simplistic. The sad truth is that most writers remain unpublished because they pay attention only to the quality of their writing. Publishers are business people. Their job is to make money from selling books. They know that high quality writing alone isn't always enough to make a profitable book, so when choosing which manuscripts to sign up for publication they think about many more elements than just the words on the page.

How to be a Writer
Secrets from the Inside
Stewart Ferris

A writer is someone who writes. It sounds obvious, but many people who call themselves writers don't produce enough words in a year to fill a postcard. Other writers churn out thousands of words but never sell their work. This book tackles both problems: it gets you writing, easily and painlessly guiding you through the dreaded 'writer's block', and it divulges industry secrets that will help you to raise the quality of your work to a professional level.

Writing is a business like any other. Successful writers know the rules and conventions that make their work stand out from the rest of the 'slush pile' – rules **Stewart Ferris** now reveals in *How to be a Writer* that will help launch your writing career.

How to be a Sitcom Writer
Secrets from the Inside
Marc Blake

TV sitcom is the goldmine genre, watched by millions. An absurd predicament, witty banter, a group of hilariously dysfunctional people: it all seems so easy. But is it? If you've ever said 'I can do better than that', then this book will encourage, test and pull you through the sitcom-writing boot camp.

How to be a Comedy Writer
Secrets from the Inside
Marc Blake

Think you're funny? Writing successful comedy isn't just about having a gift for gags; you need to hone your talent and polish your humour to earn a living from making people laugh. If you want to write stand-up comedy, sketches, sitcoms or even a comic novel or film, *How to be a Comedy Writer* tells you all you need to know and more about the business, the structure of jokes and the nuts and bolts of a craft that can be learnt.

Comedy guru **Marc Blake** has written for Spitting Image, Frankie Howerd and Craig Charles, and had his own TV show and BBC Radio 4 series Whining for England. The author of several humour books and comic novels including the bestselling Sunstroke, he has taught comedy writing across the UK for ten years.

www.summersdale.com